Stone Upon Stone

Round tower, Lusk,
Co. Dublin

Stone Upon Stone

The Use of Stone in
Irish Building

Nicholas Ryan

The Collins Press

First published in 2005 by
The Collins Press
West Link Park
Doughcloyne
Wilton
Cork
Ireland

© Nicholas Ryan
Nicholas Ryan has asserted his moral right to be identified as author of this work

British Library Cataloguing in Publication Data
Ryan, Nicholas, 1950 –
    Stone upon stone : the use of stone in Irish building
    1. Building, Stone – Ireland – History 2. Stone buildings –
    Ireland – History
    I. Title
    721' .0441
    ISBN: 1 903464 91 9

Cover photographs
Front, background image: kerbstone at Newgrange (Heritage Service of the
Department of the Environment, Heritage and Local Government);
central green band: Dún Aonghasa, Inis Mór (Heritage Service),
Trinity Church, Glendalough (Nicholas Ryan), Johnstown Castle (Heritage Service),
Millennium Wing, National Gallery (Nicholas Ryan);
bottom: Strade Abbey, Co. Mayo (Heritage Service).
Back, background image: east window at Clontuskert Abbey, Co. Galway
(Heritage Service).

Typesetting: Dominic Carroll, Co. Cork
Cover design: Peter Murphy, Oldtown Design
Printing: ColourBooks, Dublin

  Cement
Roadstone
Holdings

This publication has received support
from the Heritage Council under the
2005 Publications Grant Scheme

 The Institution
of Engineers
of Ireland

For Professor John W. de Courcy

Contents

List of Figures

Picture Acknowledgements

Figures 1, 4–5, 7–8, 10–15, 18, 23, 33–4, 36, 38–40, 42, 44, 46, 48, 50–5, 57–9, 61, 64–6, 71, 75–7, 84, 91, 94 and 100 derive from photographs of the Heritage Service of the Department of the Environment, Heritage and Local Government, with the significant assistance of Tony Roche. Figures 28–30 are taken from the nineteenth-century text, *The Book of Trades*. Figure 32 is from O'Riordan, S.P and Foy, J.B, 'The excavation of Leacanabuaile stone fort', *Journal of the Cork Historical and Archaeological Society*, vol. xlvi, no. 164, July–December 1941. Figure 47 is derived from Maurice Craig's, *The Architecture of Ireland*. Figures 60 and 79–80 are derived from *Castles and Fortifications in Ireland* by Paul M. Kerrigan. Figure 63 is courtesy of Belvedere House, Mullingar. Figure 69 is from John F. Burke's, *Outlines of the Industrial History of Ireland*. Figures 72, 81–3, 85 and 89 are from the IEI (Institution of Engineers of Ireland) archives, with the help of John Callanan. Figures 73–4 are courtesy of M.P.L. Costeloe and the Commissioners for Irish Lights. Figures 86–7 and 95–7 are from the archives of the Irish Railway Record Society, with the aid of Brendan Pender and Niall Torpey. Figure 90 is from *The Industrial Archaeology of Northern Ireland* by William A. McCutcheon. Figure 98 is from *Church of the Holy Name*, courtesy of Sheila de Courcy. Figure 103 was provided by Tom Murphy of Murphystone. I am most grateful for permission to use the above-mentioned illustrations and photographs. The remainder of the figures are my own.

Preface

Early farmers of the period around 4000 BC found that the stone they were obliged to move during field clearance was a very useful building material. The field systems of the Céide Fields in County Mayo date from about 3000 BC, and we have evidence of stone usage from that time forward. The 5–6,000 years during which we have been building in stone have left imprints in prehistory, history, culture and in folklore.

Though stone is also used in the form of gravel – as a crushed aggregate in concrete, mortar and plaster – only solid stone is considered in this volume.

A certain love of stone and stonework may be discerned, but notwithstanding this confessed bias, every effort has been made to maintain objectivity. An exception has been made when dealing with our beloved Gobán Saor, the great master mason of Irish antiquity, who is above such modern restrictions and who is allotted a final section to himself.

Acknowledgements

This publication is a development of a paper presented in February 2003 to the Heritage Society of the Institution of Engineers of Ireland. I wish to acknowledge assistance from numerous friends, colleagues and experts, and from my wife Wyn and my family, all of whom have been very generous with advice, information, inspiration and support.

Professor John de Courcy, when he was chairman of the Heritage Society, was particularly inspirational and supportive, and was the first to suggest that I should undertake the work. Dr Ronald C. Cox, the current chairman of the Heritage Society and director of the Centre for Civil Engineering Heritage at Trinity College, Dublin, made his sources available to me; whilst he read my script and offered valuable advice for which I am most grateful, I take full responsibility for any errors or omissions in the final text.

Financial support for publication was generously provided by Cement Roadstone Holdings.

1

Prehistoric Stone Buildings

Early Builders

The earliest inhabitants of Ireland brought with them memories of their parent cultures. Their first buildings here would have been crude shelters – timber, in plentiful supply, was used as the basic structural component in dwellings – and during the period when viable communities were being established, dreams of finer things remained just dreams.

These first visitors arrived around 6000 BC, but left little evidence of their building. By contrast, the earliest farmers – who arrived about 4000 BC – left significant traces, as it was during the Neolithic period, from about 4000–2000 BC, that stone began to be used in the construction of lasting monuments. Today, there are about 1,200 known megaliths in Ireland, together with many more stone cists, which can be very simple rectilinear stone boxes, with or without a mound. The most extensive Stone Age monument in the world is found at the Céide Fields in County Mayo, where house sites, megalithic tombs and dry-stone-walled field systems have been preserved under bogland.

Megalithic Monuments

The major megalithic monument types are court tombs (numbering about 339[1]), portal tombs (numbering about 163[2]), passage graves (numbering about 300[3]) and wedge-shaped tombs (numbering about 400[4]). All are examples of stone-building technology in its infancy.

The court tombs (Figure 1) are generally constructed using large, upright, stone orthostats to define the outline of the courts, chambers and cairns, although dry-stone walling using smaller stones is also evident. The courts are generally unroofed, and the chambers are roofed using either flat stones or the corbel technique of overlapping stones. In general, the entrances from the courts to the chambers are through special jamb stones, as are the passages between the chambers. Some

Fig. 1 *Creevykeel Court Tomb, Co. Sligo*

Fig. 2 *Portal tomb at Brownshill, Co. Carlow*

also have sill stones. The cairns are about 30 metres long, varying in width from about 15 metres at the front to about 7 metres at the rear. The tomb at Creevykeel in Sligo has a fully encircled court, as can be seen at the top of the photograph in Figure 1.

Portal tombs (Figure 2) usually have large orthostats forming three sides of a trapezoidal chamber; the front can be closed off using a slightly lower stone. The whole is usually surmounted by a large capstone resting on the two sides and on the rear stone, which is set low so that the capstone soars over the entrance. The slab over the tomb at Brownshill in County Carlow is estimated to weigh around a hundred tons. Wedge-shaped tombs (Figure 3) are so called because they

Fig. 3 *Giant's Grave, Co. Dublin*

often decrease in width and height from the front inwards. The chambers, or galleries, vary in length from about 2–14 metres and are formed using large orthostats. The chambers are roofed using large stone slabs; sometimes – where an orthostat is short – it is extended with a pad-stone to match its companion on the other side of the chamber. The whole chamber is usually covered with a cairn, which can be up to 15 metres in diameter and is often contained within a kerb. The example shown in Figure 3, at Ballyedmonduff in County Dublin, is known locally as a giant's grave, and though now inside a forest, was originally to be found on an open hillside.

Passage graves (Figure 4) involve the construction of passages leading to chambers, and surrounded by cairns that can vary in diameter from about 8 metres to 85 metres and which can can rise up to 10 metres. Very often, these cairns are contained by massive orthostat kerbs, and in some cases a further circle of freestanding stones occurs. The passages and chambers are usually constructed using orthostats, as shown in Figure 4, the passages being roofed with slabs, while the chamber roof is normally of corbelled construction. Some of the passage graves

Fig. 4 *Newgrange Passage Grave, Co. Meath*

have near-vertical revetments around the entrance areas. In Newgrange, this is sitting on the kerb and is about 3 metres high. A particular feature of the Newgrange monument is that it is designed and oriented so that the rays of the rising sun shine

Fig. 5 *Corbelled roof over chamber at Knowth, Co. Meath*

right into the burial recess at the back of the chamber during the winter solstice. Because the site is sloping downwards towards the southeast, a special light box had to be constructed high above the entrance, and the space between the passage orthostats had to be high and clear.

In most cases, the stones used in the megalithic monuments are of local origin. Many, however, are of great size, and resolving the problems associated with locating and amassing suitable materials and transporting them to the site suggests admirable organisational skills. Some stones were imported from distant sources, as in, for example, the revetments at Newgrange, where the white quartz probably came from the Wicklow mountains and the grey granite from the Mourne mountains. While boulders were used as megaliths, it is also true that some quarrying took place. At Carrowmore in Sligo, granite boulders were split and the flat faces were turned inwards to form the chambers and to provide flat undersides for the roofs.[5] The ability to split stone at such an early date is surprising.

The technique for standing large stones on end is not known. In some cases, they stand on unprepared ground; in others, they are set in prepared holes where they may be wedged using smaller stones. In the Burren area, some stones were stabilised by insertion into grykes, or cracks, in the limestone pavement.[6] In many cases, the orthostats had to withstand horizontal pressures from cairn material, and though they were generally successful in fulfilling this function, some failed. It appears that the roof stones were often hauled into place at the stage when the cairn material could be used as a ramp. It is possible that the chambers and passages were temporarily filled until the roof stones were in place. In the specific case of the portal tombs, it would appear they did not have cairns; however, this may not mean that they did not have temporary backfilling to facilitate the placing of the capstones, which were often of great size. A great number of monuments have withstood not only the vertical and horizontal loads inherent in their design but also the many earth tremors to have occurred in the past 6,000 years. Others, however, have collapsed. The portal tombs rely on gravity and on adequate contact between the capstones and the orthostats, and slight misalignment or redistribution of weight – caused perhaps by settlement of one of the stones – can give rise to instability and lead to collapse.

A significant stone building capability had developed about 3200 BC when Newgrange was planned and built. The excavating archaeologist described the construction process and gave an informed commentary on the probable nature of the design, management and mobilisation deployed.[7] This included a clear plan of work that could be carried out by different groups under supervision and over a number of years. Suitable stones were collected, sorted, decorated, carefully placed in position and surrounded by a mound raised in appropriate stages and designed to avoid overstressing of vulnerable parts.

The technique used to roof the central chamber is known as corbelling: rings of stone were placed in position with each ring slightly over-sailing the one below until the remaining hole was small enough to be covered with a final stone. The stones in each corbel ring were set tightly, with vertical joints staggered. They were laid with a slight upward tilt towards the centre so that water was directed outwards. Loads from subsequent layers caused compression in the horizontal rings, which were supported on timber 'horses' until stable. The roof was caulked with a mixture of burned clay and sea sand to prevent ingress of water. Though it is tempting to see this caulking as an early mortar, it was not used as a bedding medium. The corbelled roof stones were pick-dressed to partially round off their lower edges. Some of the passages roof stones had water grooves cut into their tops to direct water percolating through the mound away from the passage. Figure 5 shows the inside of the chamber roof in Knowth passage grave, which is of similar construction.

While the Boyne Valley monuments are of importance, the evident sophistication of their builders did not develop spontaneously. Rather, one must presume that skills were acquired in the construction of stone buildings that predated these monuments. Other tombs and stone walls had been built and these should not be thought unimportant in the history of building; however, they were of significantly lesser complexity. During the Neolithic period, there is evidence of a growth in knowledge of construction involving an empirical understanding of gravitational and lateral forces, of the planning and organising of resources and crews for larger projects, and of the development of skills such as handling, lifting, corbelling, splitting and decorating stones, together with methods for weather-proofing finished structures.

While the first farmers brought with them knowledge of habitation and funerary structures from their homelands in western Europe, and the later passage-grave builders brought a different architectural repertoire that they developed in a distinctive manner,[8] it is generally held that Irish builders had little if any contact with the building traditions of Rome, Greece or Egypt in the period prior to Christianity.

Clocháns and Cashels

The next stage in the utilisation of stone as a building material began in areas where loose stone was readily available. Beehive huts (*clocháns*) of corbelled construction (Figure 6), and protective promontory forts and ringforts (*cashels* or *cathairs*; Figure 7) were developed to a high degree of sophistication with little outside influence. (It should be noted that in some parts of Ireland, the term *clochán* refers to stepping-stones

Fig. 6 *Clochán na Carraige, Inis Mór, Co. Galway*

Fig. 7 *Staigue Fort, Co. Kerry*

across a river.) Stone for *cashels* and *clocháns* came from local sources. Loose surface stones were used, but stone was also quarried from the surface layers of limestone beds. The amount of dressing employed in *cashels* and *clocháns* was minimal, but stone selection was developed to such a degree that clarity of geometrical outline was achieved.

Clochán huts may be of very early origin but their construction continued for many centuries, and they served as dwellings until recently; they are still used as outhouses in the Dingle area, where the ability to build or restore them has not been lost. Those currently studying dry-stone walling in the Drimnagh Castle project in Dublin are introduced to *clochán* construction, and there are recently constructed examples on this site. *Clocháns* have been found in association with stone forts whose origins – from about 300 BC – are usually attributed to the Iron Age, although archaeological evidence at Dún Aonghasa (Figure 8) on Inis Mór suggests that it was inhabited in the Bronze Age.

The building of stone forts and *cashels* continued well into the Christian period, although there is no evidence to suggest further building after the coming of the Normans. Dún Aonghasa was first enclosed – possibly by earthworks – about 1500 BC and remained in use until about AD 1000. During this period, the practice of stone building was applied to various additions and alterations, with the last extensive rebuilding taking place around AD 500. Though Dún Aonghasa is a promontory fort, its construction is similar to

Fig. 8 *Dún Aonghasa, Inis Mór, Co. Galway*

that of the more common circular forts, or *cashels*. Its enclosure includes a number of foundations for stone houses. A distinct characteristic of both the stone forts and the houses is the batter caused by the reduction of the inner and outer diameter as courses rise. In these basically circular structures, the batter enhances stability, with the tendency to move inwards inducing a tightening of the masonry rings. Archaeological examination has shown that the thick walls of Dún Aonghasa have three distinct walls within the cross section. Any one of these walls would have been sufficient to provide security for the occupants, though there is good reason to suspect that the *cashels* attained their spectacular size and impact due to the self-aggrandisement of petty kings. It would appear that ancient laws required subject clients to help in the construction of the ramparts about their lord's *dún*.[9] 'It is then that he is king when ramparts of vassalage surround him.'[10] Thus, the clients/tenants supplied the vassals and continued to express their loyalty in this way long after the basic needs of their lord were satisfied.

2

Stone Decoration & Sculpture

Rock Art and Megaliths

Rock art – in which designs are cut into the surface of exposed rocks – occurs in many countries and is to be found in Ireland in such places as Donegal, Louth, Dingle and the Iveragh Peninsula. Much rock art has been documented, including that of 40 locations near Sneem in County Kerry – notably Derrynablatha (Figure 9). Thought to be of Neolithic date, they may derive from, rather than predate, passage-grave art.

Builders used surface decoration on stones in the monuments of the Boyne culture, and this developed to the degree that, on some stones, much of the exposed surfaces were

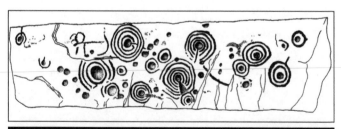

Fig. 9 *Illustration of rock art at Derrynablatha, Co. Kerry*[1]

14

Fig. 10 *Entrance kerb, Newgrange, Co. Meath*

worked. An example of this – the entrance kerbstone at Newgrange – can be seen in Figure 10. Relatively simple methods were employed to create the artwork: incised lines were used to mark out the patterns which were then more deeply incised by a picking method. It is probable that flint or quartz tools and wooden mallets formed the basic tool kit. Some of the grooves cut in the surfaces in Newgrange were smoothed using sand and water.[2] False relief, in which the area around the design is picked away, was used in the Knowth-tomb kerbstone (Figure 11) and in the roof box in Newgrange. In some cases, the whole of the glacial surface of a boulder was removed using area picking, before the incised designs were carved. Some of the more advanced designs were achieved using broad incised bands rather than grooves. Examples of this are found in the Knowth tomb.

Fig. 11 *Kerbstone at Newgrange, Co. Meath*

At around the same time, some early examples of stone worked in the round were achieved. Two fine examples have been recorded in the passage tomb at Knowth. One is a decorated basin (Figure 12) that was placed in one of the passage recesses for ceremonial purposes, and the other is a

Fig. 12 *Basin Stone at Knowth*

small mace head. Basins hollowed out of boulders were also found in other passage graves. Thus, the earliest stone sculpture is Neolithic in date.

Iron Age to Early Christian Art

Following the passage-grave builders, a culture whose monuments were dolmens and wedge-shaped graves became more prevalent; there is little evidence of stone sculpture in the period beginning around 2000 BC and continuing until stones worked in the round occur again in the Iron Age. First, we have three-faced stone heads in the fifth to first century BC,

Fig. 13 *Boa Island figure, Co. Fermanagh*

and then strange figures – thought to be of a later, Christian date – were found in Fermanagh and are now displayed on modern plinths on Boa Island (Figure 13). Both are about 70 centimetres high (some suggest a later Christian date for these). It is the La Tène pattern decorated stones at Castlestrange in Roscommon and

Fig. 14 *Turoe Stone, Co. Galway*

Turoe in Galway (Figure 14), however, that mark the arrival of mature stone sculpture in the round.

The first signs of literacy appear in Ireland around the fourth century, when – under Roman influence – pillar stones began to be inscribed with *ogham* inscriptions. These stones may have been in place earlier and are thought to be memorials or boundary markers. The inscriptions generally include the name of a person – possibly a pagan chief or tribal owner of territory – and some contain information that is clearly Christian. About one-third of the known *ogham* stones are associated with Christian foundations.

In the early Christian period, there is a return to surface

decoration of stones, and cross-inscribed slabs are found from the fifth century onwards. A slab currently displayed in Clonmacnoise (Figure 15) commemorates a craftsman; its inscription reads: 'OR DO THUATHAL SAER', meaning 'pray for Tuthal the mason' (*saer*, or *saor*, can also be translated as 'craftsman' or 'wright'.)

Fig. 15 *Craftsman's slab, Clonmacnoise, Co. Offaly*

Stone Crosses

In the seventh century AD, the rudimentary form of the Celtic cross starts to emerge from the stone. In the eighth century, these develop into the early high crosses whose surfaces are decorated with abstract patterns reminiscent of pre-existing bronze and gold artefacts. The crosses of Ahenny in County Tipperary are examples of this phase. Ninth-century high crosses tell narrative stories, with the panels used to illustrate passages from the Bible. Figure 16 shows panels on the high cross of

Fig. 16 (left) *Base of Cross of Moone, Co. Kildare*
Fig. 17 (right) *White Island figure, Co. Fermanagh*

Moone in Kildare that illustrate the stories of Adam and Eve and the Flight into Egypt.

The Cross of Muiredach in Clonmacnoise, at over 5 metres in height, was completed during the ninth to tenth centuries. The east cross, at the same site, is 6.5 metres high. Both crosses are carved from single blocks of stone.

It is suggested that there was an Iron Age and early Christian tradition of stone carving in the Lough Erne area.[3] An example of architectural stone sculpture that predates the Hiberno-Romanesque sculpture of the twelfth century is to be seen on White Island, County Fermanagh. Here, eight distinctly Christian figures were found, and have been mounted on a wall for display (one is shown in Figure 17). The maximum height is just over 1 metre, and they are thought to have come from the structure of a pulpit in the ninth to eleventh centuries.

Romanesque and Gothic Decoration

Romanesque building, dating from the ninth to twelfth centuries, saw an explosion of sculptural activity. A similarly decorative use of stone was very prominent in the construction of the Norman-inspired monasteries, as the Romanesque period gave way to the Gothic. Extraordinarily flamboyant window tracery of great strength and delicacy is the mark of the medieval stone carver, but decorative stonework for internal furnishings – such as piscine niches, credence niches, seats and sedelias – also show high artistic achievement. Decorative mouldings around windows, doors, corbels and column capitals, and the carving of heraldic shields of abbots and nobles, became commonplace. Similarly, the tombs of noble benefactors became important features of churches. One sculptor, Rory O'Tunney, signed his work on several ornate sixteenth-century tombs; a fine example of O'Tunney's work can be seen at Kilcooley Abbey where the body of Piers fitz James Oge Butler was interred in 1526. O'Tunney, it is thought, was the master of a workshop of sculptors and possibly stonemasons employed by both English and Irish patrons in the Tipperary–Kilkenny area.

A selection of decorative work is shown in the following figures: Figure 18 shows a tomb in Strade Abbey in County Mayo; Figure 19 shows an effigy of an Anglo-Norman knight in Kilfane Church, County Kilkenny; Figure 20 shows the sedelia at Holy Cross Abbey in County Tipperary; Figures 21 and 22 show window tracery in Holy Cross Abbey; Figure 23 shows internal features, including a heraldic element, in Abbey Church at Athenry, County Galway.

Fig. 18 *Tomb, Strade Abbey, Co. Mayo*

Fig. 19 (left) *Knight in Kilfane Church, Co. Kilkenny*
Fig. 20 (right) *Sedelia at Holy Cross Abbey, Co. Tipperary*

Fig. 21 *Window tracery, Holy Cross Abbey, Co. Tipperary*

Fig. 22 *Window tracery, Holy Cross Abbey, Co. Tipperary*

Fig. 23 *Abbey Church, Athenry, Co. Galway*

Carving in Castles

While the castles and keeps of the thirteenth to the seventeenth century were generally sturdy, it would appear that the owners were uninterested in ornamentation, though some decoration did occur; in Athenry, for example, a thirteenth-century castle included engaged columns with delicately carved capitals. Carved fireplaces were sometimes built in or added later, and these often had a little ornamentation. In the sixteenth century, some windows were made of wrought stones, with designs related to early manuscripts carved in low relief.[4]

Sculpture/Carving in Modern Work

From the seventeenth century onwards, as wealth and security developed, the inclusion of ornamentation was again

popular. Some of the big houses and government buildings –
such as the Customs House in Dublin – included carving and
sculptural work of high quality. Neo-Gothic sanctuary features and altar panels were widely used in the new churches,
though a lot of the carvings were imported from the marble
quarries of Italy. Funerary monuments in churches and cemeteries kept Irish craftsmen very busy. Moneyed families built
stone vaults and statuary (Figure 24), while graveyards became
crowded with 'palaces for the dead'. The modern monumental sculptor developed as the excesses of the wealthy caused
others to scramble to be just as good, and some of the product
cannot be said to have contributed much to the quality of our
stone heritage. Indeed, some of those supplying the product
knew they were pandering to poor taste. As Seamus Murphy
put it in *Stone Mad*, 'People still have the notion that a marble

Fig. 24 *'Palaces for the dead', Mount Jerome, Dublin*

Fig. 25 *Panel on Department of Industry and Commerce, Dublin*

tombstone is the last word in respectability. And, what's more, they'll pay twice the price for it.'[5]

Stone carving and statuary were included in some major Dublin buildings of the nineteenth and twentieth centuries; for example, the Pro-Cathedral, the National Library and the College of Science (now Government Buildings). The façade of the offices of the Department of Industry and Commerce in Kildare Street has a strong relief by Gabriel Hayes (Figure 25) depicting Lugh, the Celtic god of light, releasing a flight of aeroplanes as a symbol of Ireland's expanding technological sector. But the modern movement in architecture has, to a large degree, squeezed sculpture out of building. While the postmodern phase includes more in the way of ornamentation, current taste, the cost of stonework and the availability of a wider range of options have all contributed to a dearth of stone sculpture in today's building in Ireland.

3

Equipment, Men & Commerce

Iron Tools

There is no direct evidence regarding the date at which iron was introduced into stone working. The first evidence of smelting dates from the last 700 years BC, and it seems probable that the La Tène Celts, who came to Ireland around 150–100 BC, used iron tools in the manufacture of sculpture in the round for such early work as the Turoe Stone. This is by no means certain as early iron may have tended to be soft, while the qualities of bronze tools depended upon more easily controlled constituents. The earliest date for iron chisels from the archaeological record is in the medieval period – around AD 600.[1] A single iron punch was found in the chamber of a Neolithic passage grave at Loughcrew, but it is thought that the chamber may have been used as a workshop at a later date.[2]

Mortar

Mortar is used primarily to bed and seal masonry. The caulking of the roof stones of the main chamber of Newgrange with a mixture of sea sand and burnt-clay putty cannot be considered the first recorded use of mortar but does indicate early knowledge of the fact that such mixtures of materials possessed useful qualities. If such mixtures were used for bedding or caulking right into the Christian period, they appear to have been washed away – one would scarcely expect otherwise. While the literature exhibits a marked reluctance to put a firm date on the introduction of lime mortar as we now understand it, it is thought that it occurred somewhere between the sixth and ninth centuries AD. Radiocarbon dating carried out on mortar carbonate – in which the age of cosmogonic carbon derived from the atmosphere at the time of setting was measured – resulted in a somewhat tentative set of dates for early church buildings.[3] A sample from High Island Oratory in Galway yields AD 430–852, while another from the same site yields AD 810–1020. O'Keeffe and Simington give good details of the historical development of mortar in Ireland, while Pavia and Bolton give data on the history of mortars but do not add much to the knowledge of particularly Irish mortars. Whatever the date of development or of adaptation of known practice elsewhere, mortar has played an important role in stone building from Ireland's early Christian period.

Explosives

Gunpowder became available for artillery in Ireland in 1488, but its first recorded use in mining occurred in Hungary in 1627, and it was used in the tin mines in Cornwall in 1689. Inserted into existing cracks to loosen masses of rock, the process was not very useful in the provision of building stone. The technology of drilling using long chisels (jumpers) and sledgehammers had evolved by 1637,[4] and this made it possible to predetermine the location and depth at which charges could be set so as to produce building stone of more useful dimensions. Alfred Nobel invented dynamite in the middle of the nineteenth century, and a relevant treatise on the use of explosives in quarrying by Burgoyne became available in 1874. It tells of gunpowder being introduced to quarrying in 'a comparatively recent period', and gives an interesting account of the drilling and blasting process as recorded in the granite quarries of Dalkey in County Dublin:

> 3-inch jumpers, used in boring holes from 9 to 15 feet deep; 2 men striking, and 1 man holding and turning the jumper, bored on average 4 feet in a day or 5 feet with a $2^1/_2$-inch jumper, which was frequent used for boring the same depth.[5]

Manual drilling by jumper for the extraction of building stone by explosives continued into the twentieth century in tandem with the development of explosive technology. By 1955, only gelignite was used, but significant advances in explosives and in their handling and detonation have taken place since then.[6]

Masons and Stonecutters
Each phase of colonisation/settlement brought knowledge

and skills that modified the indigenous social system to some degree. Phases in stonework were certainly influenced by imported knowledge. Christian influences are evident from St Patrick onwards, and it is said that he brought masons with him. According to the Book of Lecan:

> His three Masons, good was their intelligence,
> Caeman, Cruithnech, Luchraid strong;
> They made damliachs [stone churches] first
> In Erin; eminent their history.[7]

It is possible that these three introduced some elements of Roman practice.

The Norse people who settled in Dublin and other river estuaries from 840 onwards were not noted for stone working. Their traditional building medium was timber and wattle. Nevertheless, a stone wall was erected around part of Dublin before the Normans came, and excavations have shown some use of flagstones in the early twelfth century.

When the Normans arrived, they carried with them not only knowledge from their homeland but more exotic knowledge acquired during their expansive forays into southern Europe and on their crusades into the East, including Jerusalem. Captured Saracen craftsmen, with experience of the great buildings of Islam, are thought to have contributed significantly to Norman development.[8]

Masons were important people in most societies, but the term mason does not necessarily imply stone since it applied to builders in general. Throughout mainland Europe during medieval times, stonemasons became well organised as stone building developed. They were educated, mainly in Latin, and were trained through apprenticeships and journeying before becoming masters. Strict requirements were laid down regarding the title 'master', which we can today interpret as 'architect'. One German ordinance of 1514[9] shows that a journeyman had to make six masterworks in order to graduate:

1. A simple quadripartite vault;
2. A stone doorway of pieces;
3. A simple gateway;
4. A projection or profile (i.e., a cornice);
5. Foundation walls for a house, and where a wall or corner has become damaged to repair the wall and know how to mend it;
6. To know from the height of any wall its proper thickness and how to make an adequate foundation for it.

Stonemasons were required to be of exemplary character and of legitimate birth. They were not allowed to have concubines.

In the Roman Empire, bridges were essential. Timber predominated, but a significant number of bridges were of stone and many of these are still standing. *Pont* is the Roman word for bridge, and the priests involved in building and maintaining bridges belonged to the *Collegium Pontifices*. The head of this group was called *Pontifex Maximus,* meaning 'the greatest maker of bridges'. The social and political significance of this person is illustrated by the fact that his title was coveted by the emperors and later by the Pope.[10] In early Christian times, monks known as *Fratres Pontifices* (brothers of the bridge) built and maintained bridges, ferries and hostels for travellers in various parts of Europe. Although Irish monasteries were often built beside rivers and close to extant bridges, there is no direct evidence connecting Irish monks with similar activities. That said, the early Irish Church was known to use the title *Summus Pontifex* (highest maker of bridges) for its abbots.[11]

During the great Gothic cathedral-building period, the coveting of the status of master mason took another form. The organisations of speculative masonry, or Freemasonry, gave dignitaries an opportunity to learn about the great secrets or mysteries of the mason's trade, and led to the establishment of lodges where the theories and techniques were studied and shared within a fraternity. The secrets appear to have been based largely on the complex geometrical knowledge necessary to devise not only the overall design of such buildings but also the precise shape of each stone intended for assembly. From early times, stonemasons, in common with other craftsmen, were given a personal mark when they became journeymen, and this practice was adopted by the Freemasons. A 'mark-book' of 1781 from the Waterford lodge, containing the marks of the brothers, is extant in the library of the Grand Lodge in Molesworth Street, Dublin.

The practice of leaving a mason's mark on finely wrought stone appears to date from about the twelfth century, and seems not to have died out until the Georgian period; at Carton House, for instance, there is a mark on most of the external stones. Perhaps this practice was forbidden as the marks were a significant interference with otherwise pristine stone façades. Thereafter, many could still be found on the bedding surfaces,[12] on less-visible stones and on masonry in more utilitarian structures, such as bridges and retaining walls. These marks make it possible to follow the movement of a mason from site to site, though the identity of the mason is not generally known.

The marks of the medieval mason tend to include simple geometrical shapes as well as designs such as leaves, interlacing and fleur-de-lis,[13] those of the seventeenth and eighteenth centuries were largely confined to simple linear shapes, initials and Roman

Fig. 26 *Mason's marks*

numerals.[14] Figure 26 shows a rubbing of a mason's mark from the fifteenth-century Franciscan friary at Kilconnell, County Galway (top), and a plaster cast of a mason's mark from the bed of a stone in the eighteenth-century Custom House, Dublin (bottom). The leitmotiv of Kilconnell – carved in outline using a sharp chisel, its inner portion finished using a point tool – contrasts with the linear design at the Custom House, which was cut with a sharp chisel in a letter-cutting action.

In the period since the Normans, there is evidence that stonemasons from overseas came here to work with local masons on ecclesiastical and defence buildings. There is also evidence to suggest that Irish masons travelled through Europe to work on church-building projects. For instance, it is thought on the basis of historical and stylistic evidence that the Romanesque doorway of St Emmeram's Church in Regensburg in Bavaria may be the work of the same west of Ireland man who built the slype doorway in the Augustinian abbey at Cong in County Mayo.[15]

As with the English word 'mason', the Irish word for mason – *saor* – was not specific until given an appendage; for example, *saor cloiche* (stonemason), *saor adhmaid* (carpenter) and *saor báid* (boatwright). These *saor* people were of great importance in Irish society. In modern times, the word *saor* means 'free', but of old, it dealt with a particular level of freedom or nobility. In the Brehon Laws, the '*sóer-named* [free-privileged] classes are scholars, Churchmen, nobles and poets . . . this nobility was purchased by art rather than birth.

Honour-price [*dire*] equal to that of the lowest grade of the nobility is granted to these masons', and when they practice more than one skill, their nobility is enhanced: 'Whose art is one, his *dire* is one. Whose art is multiple, his *dire* is multiple.'[16] Thus, a mason capable of building in a multiple of disciplines could be a very important person indeed. We may also conjecture that masons practiced the skills of stonecutting as well as building in Ireland as long as the Brehon Laws held sway – that is, up until the seventeenth century. There are few named masons in the early history of building in Ireland, but there is a substantial folklore, with many of the tales relating to a fabulous mason called the *Gobán Saor*.

Early crafts in general were practiced as a family trade, and – in an informal apprenticeship – young boys worked with their fathers to learn the business. An apprenticeship to a mason was the normal way in which a boy could enter the stone crafts with the right to becoming a mason – a right often confined to the descendants of established masons. This 'closed trade' practice continued in Ireland until the introduction in the 1980s of formalised training schemes under FÁS (the Training and Employment Authority). The practice of binding boys to a master for the purpose of learning a trade developed in the medieval period; in Ireland, bound apprenticeship continued well into the twentieth century, and the conditions of these apprenticeships were agreed to and sworn out in the presence of a peace commissioner. An example of such an agreement – entered into by John O'Donohue who, in later life, became the general secretary of the stonecutters' union – is shown in Figure 27. The apprentice, his father, the master and the peace commissioner signed this document, and it was largely honoured until Mr O'Donohue became a fully fledged stonecutter.

> This Indenture Witnnesseth That John Joseph O'Donohue, aged 15 years . . . of his own free Will and Accord, and with the Consent of his Father, John O'Donohue . . . doth put himself Apprentice to Sir Simon W. Maddock, Proprietor, Mount Jerome Monumental Works, Dublin, to learn his Art, and with him (after the manner of an Apprentice), to dwell and serve, from the seventh day of November 1921 until the full End and Term of seven years to 7th. November 1928, from thence next following, be fully complete and ended; during which Term the said Apprentice his said Master faithfully shall serve, his Secrets keep, his lawful commands everywhere gladly do. He shall do no damage to his said Master nor see it to be done by others, but that he to his Power shall let or forthwith give warning to his said Master of the same. He shall not waste the goods of his said Master nor give or lend them unlaw-fully to any. He shall not commit Fornication, nor contract Matrimony within the said term. Hurt to his said Master he shall not do, or cause or procure it to be done by others. He shall not

play at Cards, Dice Tables, or any other unlawful game whereby his said Master may have Loss with his own or others' Goods during said Term. Without license of his said Master he shall neither

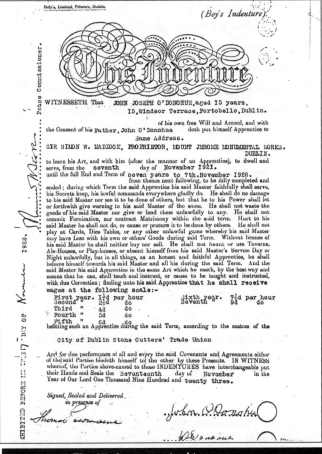

Fig. 27 *An apprenticeship agreement*

buy nor sell. He shall not haunt or use Taverns, Ale-Houses, or Play-Houses, or absent himself from his said Master's Service Day or Night unlawfully, but in all things, as an honest and faithful Apprentice, he shall behave himself towards his said Master and all his during the said Term. And the said Master his said Apprentice in the same Art which he useth, by the best way and means he can, shall teach and instruct, or cause to be taught and instructed, with due Correction; finding unto his said Apprentice that he shall receive wages at the following scale:-

First year	1^{1}/2d per hour
Second year	2^{1}/2d per hour
Third year	4d per hour
Fourth year	5d per hour
Fifth year	6d per hour
Sixth year	7^{1}/2d per hour
Seventh year	9d per hour

befitting such an Apprentice during the said Term, according to the custom of the City of Dublin Stone Cutters' Trade Union. And for due performance of all and every the said Covenants and Agreements either of the said Parties bindeth himself to the other by these Presents. In witness whereof, the Parties above-named to

these indentures have interchangeable put their
Hands and Seals the seventeenth day of November
in the Year of Our Lord One Thousand Nine
Hundred and twenty three.

Many crafts made efforts to protect the so-called 'secrets
of the trade', and what better way to achieve this than to
devise a language with which they could speak to one another
while excluding the uninitiated. The Irish stonemasons had
a language of their own called *Berlagair na Sáer*.[17] The
meaning of this term is literally 'the vernacular of the mason',
and it seems to have been a special use of Irish with some
extra devices, such as inversion of words and rhyming slang.
In use up until the nineteenth century, some of the words are
listed below, with English translations:

caid	stone
airig caide	stonemason
cadth soukeness	corner stone
pumpa	scaffold
bochar	mason's square
borbín	labourer
casar	hammer
fórúch	foreman
glaidín	knife

In recent history, the processing of stone entailed extraction
by the quarry-man (Figure 28), shaping by the stonecutter

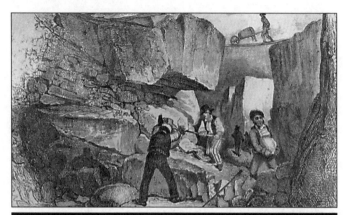

Fig. 28 *The quarry-man*

(Figure 29) and building by the mason. The people who carried out fine carving were usually called stone carvers; they were stonecutters with a flair for carving. Sculptors who worked in stone served both the monumental industry and building industry. In the early days, these tasks were the remit of the master mason, but were later separated to facilitate specialisation and to enhance efficiency. It is not known when this took place in Ireland, but a code of by-laws established in London in 1356 divided the masons into two classes: hewers and light masons, or setters.[18] This distinction held sway in Ireland late into the twentieth century, and can still give rise to demarcation disputes. In the early twentieth century, the introduction of stone-working machinery such as saws gave rise to stonecutters specialising in various mechanical skills, and towards the middle of the same century, the widespread use of stone cladding led to the need for 'fixer' skills, and again some stonecutters became specialised in this area.

In the city of Dublin, the various crafts had fraternities or brotherhoods – later called guilds – and these controlled the city corporation. Prince John granted a charter to the city of Dublin in 1192 that permitted the formation of all 'reasonable' guilds, though the earliest record of a masons' guild in Dublin is from 1513 when the masons participated in a guild with the millers and helliers (slaters). Within the stonemasons' fraternities, one master and his journeymen could constitute a lodge, a system that made for easy control by the master but which led to difficulties when men began to seek

Fig. 29 *The stonecutter*

a fairer share of the lodge's earnings. Furthermore, the weilding of political power led to corrupt guilds. Membership of the craft guilds was intended to be for craftsmen only, but membership rights were hereditary and sons who no longer practiced the craft held onto membership for the status and power it bestowed. The guilds collapsed in disrepute in the 1840s following the passing of an Act that gave voting rights in elections to all owners of property rated at over £10 per year; the influence of the guilds was thus diminished. The last masons' guild in Dublin was the guild of St Bartholomew, and in 1840 less than half of its members were craftsmen. Out of a membership of 104, a total of 65 were not masons; among the non-masons were businessmen, a viscount, a hatter, a clergyman and the inspector of prisons.[19]

The formation of trade unions had been forbidden under the Combination Acts, which were not fully repealed until 1824–25. In 1833, the Union of Bricklayers and Plasterers was established; its first chairman was Benjamin Pemberton, a mentor who had failed to reform the guild when he became its master in 1812. With the decline of the guilds, building employers needed new representative associations, prompting the establishment of quarry-owners' associations and the Dublin Master Builders' Association (DMBA), representing the interests of stone producers and masons respectively. The DMBA was revived in 1895, the countrywide Master Builders' Association was established about 1926 and the Irish House Builders' Association dates from about 1931. In 1935, the associations saw the benefit of federation and the Federation of Builders, Contractors and Allied Employers of Ireland was born. By 1943, it was an umbrella body representing master builders, master plasterers, master tilers, master glaziers and master plumbers. Renamed the Construction Industry Federation, it now incorporates 37 specialist associations, including the Architectural and Monumental Stone Association.

Use of the term 'mason' has declined in much of Ireland, but it is still used in southern regions from around Waterford southwards. In the Dublin region, the layers are known as 'bricklayers', and they lay bricks, concrete blocks and stone. Stonecutters are not normally allowed to construct stonework on union-controlled sites, but it is accepted that they can fix stone cladding. From time to time – when demand is high – the masons' unions provide temporary union cards to stone-cutters to allow them to participate in building work.

In the early twentieth century, masons were members of the brick and stone layers' unions. The Stonecutters' Union of Ireland was formed in Cork in 1848, moving its head-quarters to Dublin in 1898. The rules of the stonecutters' union were reminiscent of those of the guild lodges:

> The Society shall be constituted by Lodges organ-ised in towns or districts where members are employed; each Lodge shall consist of not less than five members; that to which, for the time being, the management is entrusted to be called the Central Lodge.[20]

The union representing stoneworkers in the mid-twentieth century was the Ancient Guild of Incorporated Brick and Stone Layers' Trade Union. In reality, it was neither a guild nor very ancient, having been formed in 1959. The bricklayers amalgamated with the carpenters at the end of the 1980s, and together with the stone workers are now represented in negotiations by the Building and Allied Trades' Union.

Stonework is now only a small component of general building, and masons/bricklayers far outnumber stonecutters. Nevertheless, the training of bricklayers still includes elements of stone laying. The formal training of stonecutters is now undertaken at the FÁS Training Centre in Tralee, while dry-stone-walling trainees are instructed through FÁS at Drimnagh Castle in Dublin. The construction and improvement of major national roads during the last decade has been accompanied by the building of many miles of random rubble walls by a combination of masons, bricklayers and stonecutters, among them workers from overseas.

Stone-working Equipment

Up until the twentieth century, there was little development of tools and machinery for stone masonry. With the exception of the use of explosives, stone was extracted using techniques that could be traced back to the building of the Pyramids. Stone was cut and dressed with hammers, mallets and chisels whose design was likewise ancient, though iron was to replace bronze as the material from which the tools were made, and steel would later replace iron. The ancient saws for the cutting of various soft stones were used in Irish quarries until comparatively recently; Figure 30, a woodcut, shows a marble cutter in operation.

Marble was hand polished up to the 1740s, when it is recorded that water-powered cutting and polishing was in

Fig. 30 *The marble cutter*

use in the Kilkenny quarries.[21] There is little evidence of anything other than hand polishing in smaller establishments or in sculptors' workshops until the twentieth century. Items like squares, plumb bobs, compasses, hods and trowels are also ancient. Lifting devices, both in the quarry and on site, employed block and tackle, simple cranes, crabs and pulleys.

Though originally timber in construction, it seems probable that improvements were made to these devices around the early nineteenth century, following the late-eighteenth-century development of cast iron.

Engines for driving cranes were probably not deployed in the Irish building industry until the twentieth century; a steam crane was certainly in operation in a granite quarry at Ballycorus in County Dublin in the 1920s. In general, mechanisation did not really happen in the Irish stone industry until rural electrification in the 1940s. In this decade, frame saws appeared; these could produce flat slabs for paving as well as architectural stone. The frame saws were followed by wire saws in which helical-grooved wire, fed with grit, is pulled across the stone like a cheese cutter. In 1948, a Czechoslovakian mechanical engineer, Arpad Roth, arrived in Ireland as a refugee. Experienced with stone-working machinery, Roth went into business with James Murphy, a Dublin quarry owner. The firm, Sandyford Engineering, producing saws, polishers, grinders and other devices for the stone industry, both here and abroad.

Industrial-diamond technology led to the development of circular saws with diamond tips, and these too were manufactured here and exported overseas. Soon, primary circular saws capable of cutting depths of over 1 metre were in use, and smaller-diameter saws were used for sizing the resulting slabs. The circular saws could be fixed to a frame, and lowered and advanced manually with continuous water cooling. Later, they were automated and could be programmed to run 24 hours a day if necessary. Smaller blades – down to 100 millimetres in diameter – running on flexible drives were used for detailed work until the introduction into the trade of the angle grinder in the 1980s.

The mechanisation of extraction also advanced. Jackhammers, utilising compressed-air technology, became available towards the end of the nineteenth century, and gradually came into use for building-stone extraction in the first half of the twentieth century. Mechanised drilling rigs began to be used in the 1950s, and are now capable of producing very accurate hole patterns. Environmental and safety concerns have led to improvement in the control of noise and dust, and the days of long hours of hard manual graft have passed into history.

Precision drilling allowed wire saws with diamond-embedded studs to be fed vertically down a quarry face to an intercepting horizontal hole, and be drawn under tension so as to slice a clean, vertical cut. Very large blocks can be extracted in this way without the damaging effects of explosives. A technology developed for the marble quarries of Carrera in Italy, it was introduced to Irish limestone quarries in the 1970s, though it took a further twenty years to perfect a system suitable for use in granite quarries, granite being markedly harder than limestone.

The facility to produce large blocks was enhanced by the introduction of thermal-lance cutting in the 1970s, but this process has not found widespread favour. In very recent times, diamond-tipped chainsaws have been developed.

Originally intended for the concrete industry, they are proving useful in the working of soft stone; it is expected that they will soon be made suitable for harder stone.

In the second half of the twentieth century, mechanically achieved surface finishes became feasible, such as bush hammered, machine chiselled, ribbed, acid etched, sawn and flame textured.

Growing awareness of the dangers of silicosis has led to the introduction of mechanical dust extraction and the use of particulate masks, but many lethal cases have occurred over the years.

Calculation of Masonry Sizes

Stone walls subject to horizontal pressure came under scientific scrutiny around 1687 when the French General Vauban developed his sliding-prism theory. Coulomb, another French officer, improved on the original theory around 1773, and Professor Rankine deduced his more subtle theory in 1856. Refinement in the general area of geotechnics has continued since that time. Engineers, among them the eminent Richard Castle – who arrived in Ireland in 1728 – were familiar with the application of numerical methods to retaining walls.

The story of the analysis and design of stone arches goes back further. The fourteenth-century Italian Renaissance saw the construction of Brunelleschi's dome over the cathedral of Florence, and with it the application of scientific method to building for the first time. The problem of the mathematical design of bridges was given a fillip in 1675 when Robert Hook declared that 'as hangs the flexible line, so but inverted will stand the rigid arch'. In 1675, David Gregory stated that 'none but the cateneria is the figure of the true legitimate arch' and 'when an arch of any other figure is supported, it is because in its thickness some cateneria is included'.[22] There were experiments involving the hanging of representative loads on suspended strings to determine the possible shapes of arches and the relationship between shape, loading and abutment thrusts. After this, the application of the funicular polygon to solve the forces in an arch became possible. In 1748, G. Poleni used this idea in his analysis of the cracked dome of St Peter's when he considered the dome as if it were composed of 50 segments. He found the actual shape of his catenary by loading a flexible string with weights proportional to that supported by each segment of the arches, and showed that his experimental line of thrust did lie within the thickness of the arch. In this way, he also deduced experimentally the value of the horizontal thrust at the base of the dome and confirmed the need for additional ties to sustain this thrust.[23] P. de La Hire resolved the issue of the stability of arch and pier in 1695, and this led in 1712 to the publication of work by B.F. de Bélidor in 1729, and to memoirs on arch thrust by P. Couplets in 1729 and 1730.[24] Because of the growing knowledge and the importance of roads and bridges, the Corps des Ponts et Chaussées (bridges and roads) was established in Paris in 1716, followed by the Ecole (school) des Ponts et Chaussées in 1747, with Jean R. Perronet as its inaugural director. He was the first to apply the knowledge that the intermediate piers, in a multi-span bridge of equal spans, carry little horizontal thrust and can thus be reduced in width, as in the Pont de Neuilly in 1768–74.

W.H. Barlow, C.A.P. Castigliano and Y. Villarceau pioneered further important experimental and analytical steps in the nineteenth century and, as a result, engineers were provided with a set of tables and standard calculations that could be used in bridge design.[25] The art of stone arch-bridge design, then, was developed from the fifteenth to the nineteenth century; it is still developing, though mainly for the purpose of assessment and maintenance. In the table of stone bridges given in O'Keeffe and Simington, four are pre-Norman, twelve are of the twelfth to thirteenth centuries, 22 are from the fourteenth to sixteenth centuries, and 28 are of the seventeenth to eighteenth centuries. Irish stone arches were probably subjected to calculation from the eighteenth century onwards. Still in existence are partially corbelled arch bridges, with only the top third of the arch composed of radially jointed work; though this may represent a development of the roof-corbelling technique predating the twelfth century, some authorities consider it improbable that significant stone bridges were built in Ireland before the coming of the Cistercians in 1148 and the Normans in 1169.[26]

Clapper bridges – composed of stone slabs supported on stone piers – were reasonably common and some still exist. The largest extant, near Buttevant in County Cork, contains a limestone slab measuring 2.85 metres by 1.2 metres by 180 millimetres.

The thickness of walls subject to vertical load was originally derived empirically, and there are many references in Europe to unsuccessful efforts – resulting in collapse – during the Gothic adventure. This empirical knowledge was passed on to stonemasons during training, and though scientific method was well established since the eighteenth century, the complex issue of the relationship between the strengths of mortars and masonry units and the load-bearing capacity of these elements in walls of varying height, length and restraint remains a matter of international debate. London has had regulations covering the thickness of such walls since the twelfth century. Thickness was a matter of prescription right up to the early years of the twentieth century, and though the regulations appear to have been based on experience rather than calculation, there may have been some element of scientific method in drawing them up. Figure 31 shows the

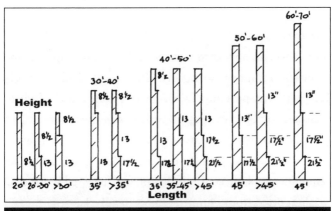

Fig. 31 *London County Council prescribed wall thickness*

method of assessing prescribed wall thickness based on the London County Council construction by-laws of 1937. Under London's 1908 General Powers Act, infill panels of lesser thickness were permitted to facilitate the growth in steel framing where the enforcement of old prescribed thickness methods had resulted in unnecessary waste. In 1937, London by-laws permitted for the first time calculation on the basis of strength designations and permissible pressures. The old prescribed-thickness approach continued, and still exists as an option in British building regulations. The prescription of wall thickness was a feature of Irish practice until the demise of the by-laws and introduction of Proposed Building Regulations in the 1970s. While the practice of numerical analysis – based on CP 111, the code of practice for load-bearing walls first issued in 1948 – had been commonplace, it was applied mainly to brickwork and blockwork, and was seldom used for stonework.

Trade in Stone

The Normans appear to have been the first to import stone – the Caen stone of Normandy. Given the difficulties associated with transportation by road, Caen stone was used where transport by boat was feasible, such as in the windows and internal arches in St Mary's Abbey, New Ross and at other sites. The Normans also used a fine, yellow, oolite limestone from Dundry Hill, south of Bristol, and 'new red sandstone' was imported from Dumfries in Scotland.

Wren's use of Portland stone when rebuilding London

after the fire of 1666 made it fashionable, and it was widely used here during the Georgian period. In the eighteenth century, limestone was imported from the south of England for important buildings such as Castletown, Cashel Palace and Waterford Cathedral. Bath stone was also imported; among other projects, it was used for the building of Castleward in County Down. Coade stone – an artificial stone – was imported from London from the 1750s, and used on the Rutland Fountain and on the frieze of the Rotunda Hospital.[27] Kilkenny limestone/marble was exported from the middle of the eighteenth century to places such as Bristol, Liverpool, London and Glasgow. A fine-grained, red limestone/marble from around Donaghy's Cross near Midleton in County Cork was used in the Catholic Cathedral of Westminster and at St Pancras' Station in London. The modern industry actively seeks contracts overseas and has exported stone to as far away as the United States of America.

The Irish slate industry is long established but has never been large. In 1844, Sir Robert Kane noted the existence of a handful of small concerns: at Broadford in County Clare, Westport in County Mayo, Ross in County Wexford, Clonakilty and Kinsale in County Cork, and near Rathdrum in County Wicklow. There were only three enterprises of more than minor importance: quarries at Glassmore employed 100 people; on Valentia Island about 200 people were employed; at Killaloe in County Limerick about 700 men and boys were employed. During the 1840s, the Killaloe operation had an annual output of around 10,000 tons of manufactured slate. Nevertheless, Slate continued to be imported; in the 1870s, 'Eureka green slate' from the US was used for the roofing of Christ Church Cathedral. Subsequently, imported slate from the US performed poorly in the Dublin weather and lost its share of the market.

Most Irish quarries were remote from the main centres of demand, and Welsh slate companies were able to compete on price due to greater economies of scale and the ability to transport by sea. In 1896–97, a trade dispute in Wales affected production, but as the Irish quarries were not in a position to make up the shortfall, the demand was largely met by US slates.[28]

In 1904 – the first year for which there are statistics from the Central Statistics Office (CSO) – the total quantity of building and monumental stone imported into Ireland (32 counties) was about 42,000 tonnes, and the total exports amounted to about 62,000 tonnes. In 2003, the last year for which current statistics are available, Ireland (26 counties) imported about 44,600 tonnes and exported about 3,500 tonnes. During the 1930s and 1940s, there was little move-ment of stone – imports or exports – but trade improved during the 1950s, and both imports and exports increased significantly from the 1970s.

In 1904, imports of stone were entirely from Britain, while exports were listed in CSO statistics as 'to Great Britain and places abroad'. The value of imports in 1904 was about £152,000, two-thirds of which was for slate. Exports were worth about £18,000, of which around 80 per cent was setts, kerbs and paving. The current value of imports is running at about €15.8 million and exports at around €2 million; the bulk of exports is to the Belgian market. Setts, kerbs and paving are a very small part of exports, but comprise around 20 per cent of imports.

In recent years, stone has been imported from a wide range of countries. Slate came from Argentina, Belgium, Brazil, Britain, China, France, Germany, Italy, Northern Ireland, Portugal and Spain. Other stone – mainly marble and granite – comes from those countries listed above and from Bolivia, Chile, Egypt, Finland, Greece, Hong Kong, Indonesia, Iran, Italy, Japan, Lebanon, Malaysia, New Zealand, Norway, Pakistan, South Africa, Sweden, Thailand, US, Vietnam and Zimbabwe. Irish stone is exported to Belgium, Britain, China, France, Germany, Japan, Morocco, the Netherlands, Northern Ireland, South Africa and the US.

4

Early Christian Period to the Thirteenth Century

Early Houses

The circle would appear to have been the preferred shape of the early Irish house, whether of wood or stone, although some evidence of very primitive rectangular houses has been found. The earliest *clocháns* were circular both inside and outside, and it was not until the Christian period that they started to become rectangular. Clochán na Carraige, on Inis Mór, is of roughly rectangular plan inside and oval outside. It has internal dimensions of about 6 metres by 2.4 metres by 2.5 metres high. Walls over 1 metre thick at the base give an external oval plan shape of about 8 metres by 4.5 metres. It features two doors in opposing walls and one narrow window; it has no other exit for smoke. Its rough external shape and the presence of projecting stones lead to the theory that it was originally covered with thatch or with earthen sods.

Some early medieval houses of stone were not of the corbelled type or were only corbelled for a portion of their height, over which they were thatched. At Leacanabuaile in Kerry, a stone ringfort of about 21 metres internal diameter

– excavated in 1939–40 – was found to contain one circular house and three rectangular houses of later date.[1] It is thought that the round house dates from about the seventh century AD, while the eleventh or twelfth century is suggested for the rectangular houses. Evidence from other sites suggests that the change from round to square took place around the eighth century.[2] The circular house at Leacanabuaile was about 5 metres in internal diameter, with walls 1.5 metres thick. These walls rose vertically to 1.2 metres and corbelled to 1.7 metres in height. Post-holes in the floor suggested that

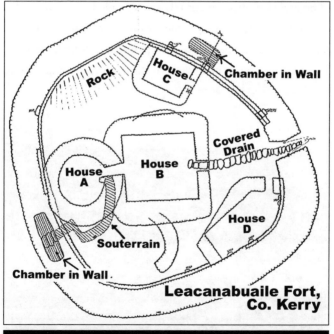

Fig. 32 *Leacanabuaile stone fort, Co. Kerry*

the roof was timbered and thatched from some height above this. The main rectangular house is 7.1 metres by 6.1 metres internally, with walls up to 1.8 metres thick. These walls survive to 1.5 metres in height, and it is not known if corbelling occurred above this, though the existence of postholes indicates the probability of a thatched roof. Figure 32 shows the whole site at Leacanabuaile. There are other interesting features, including a subterranean passage – or *souterrain* – drains and hidden chambers inside the walls.

Early Christian Stone Churches

The earliest Christian churches were called *dairtheach* – literally 'oak house'. Some of these timber structures were quite large, and highly decorated and painted.[3] At the same time, the *clochán* – made of stone – continued in use and began to

Fig. 33 Monastic settlement, Scelig Mhichíl, Co. Kerry

grow in size and complexity. The 'huts' on Scelig Mhichíl off the Kerry coast (Figure 33) measure up to 9 metres in diameter and 5.5 metres in height, and include features like cupboards and cantilevered peg stones for hanging manuscript satchels.

Early timber churches were rectangular, and it was not long before the *clocháns* became rectangular inside while remaining dome-like outside. The next step was to create rectangularity both inside and outside, and this was achieved with some success. The structural principle required the use of walls of great thickness – often up to about 2 metres – and required no mortar.

From the seventh century onwards, churches and their associated buildings and cemeteries were grouped in areas surrounded by ramparts of earthworks or stone. At the sixth-century foundation of St Mochaoi in Nendrum, County Down, for example, there are three more-or-less concentric enclosures. The inner enclosure is about 76 metres in diameter and has a stone wall about 2 metres thick. A stone church, a later round tower and a cemetery are sited in the central area, while the second enclosure contains the foundations of circular and rectangular houses. In some cases, the building of these ramparts was crude, but some of them were well faced with stone and had significant gateways.

The earliest reference to a stone church – or *damliac* – is from AD 724; it gave its name to Duleek, the village in County Meath where it was built.[4] In 789, another stone church is mentioned in Armagh,[5] but there is no reference to any other stone church until the tenth century. The Annals tell us that Abbot Colmán built a stone church in 909 under the patronage of Flann Sinna, high king of the Uí Néill at Clonmacnoise; a panel in one of the high crosses shows the king and abbot planting a ceremonial stake, probably indicating mutual respect between Church and state.[6]

The stone church at Tuamgreiney and its *cloigtheach* – or round tower – was built by Abbot Cormac, who died in 964.[7] The majority of references to churches in the Annals relate to timber constructions up to 965, but stone becomes more important thereafter.[8] These churches were mainly small, timber-roofed, single-celled buildings ranging from about

Fig. 34 *Teampall Bheanáin, Inis Mór, Co. Galway*

5–10.5 metres in length; they generally faced west. The walls were about 1 metre in thickness and were often faced with large, well-cut slabs and filled with rubble set in mortar, as at Teampall Bheanáin on Inis Mór (Figure 34). In this case, the plan size is about 4.6 metres by 3.5 metres. Eventually, the single-celled buildings were developed to include a chancel, often accessed through a fine, semicircular arch. Such an arch can be seen in the pre-Romanesque Trinity Church at Glendalough, County Wicklow (Figure 35). These arches were very striking though without decoration, and they were later to provide a challenge for the Romanesque carvers.

The earliest stone churches had small, rectangular windows and doors with sloping jambs, a feature shared with the Greeks and the Romans from an early date. Doors hung in such openings would have been self-closing. The door at

Fig. 35 *Trinity Church, Glendalough, Co. Wicklow*

St Kevin's Kitchen in Glendalough is such a door, and features, unusually, a relieving arch in the stonework overhead. There are numerous references to stone churches in existence or being built in the eleventh and twelfth centuries, and the protective stone walls and gateways to both monastic centres and trading towns – such as Glendalough and Dublin – were becoming an important element in the work of the mason.

West doors in pre-Romanesque stone churches often have large lintels, architraves in relief and a little decoration. An example can be seen at the church in Fore, County Westmeath (Figure 36), which features a main door of well-dressed stone slightly decreasing in width as it rises. The door head is a good example of a large monolithic lintel: it is huge and forms part of a raised surround, and also has a cross-in-circle decoration. Because of its size, the lintel at Fore is traditionally known as one of the 'Seven Wonders of Fore'.

As doors were beginning to display some decoration, window heads also began to develop. They became semi-circular with the curve cut from two blocks corbelled from each jamb; later, they were carved from a single stone lintel. Soon, the window jambs and sill were formed in worked stone, and simple ornamentation followed. Thus was born the style 'Hiberno-Romanesque', although many authorities consider this an overly grand title. One of the windows in Reefert Church at Glendalough, County Wicklow (Figure 37) shows this development. The external window head is cut from a single stone, and the wider internal ope is now formed of fine-granite cut stone, while the wall remains mica-schist rubble.

At its height, the Romanesque influence led to significant semicircular arches in doors, windows and opes between internal spaces, and to great stone columns, piers, carvings and fine ashlar work on the external surfaces. Cormac's Chapel at Cashel in County Tipperary (Figure 38) is probably the best

Fig. 36 *Doorway at Fore, Co. Westmeath*

Fig. 37 *Window in Reefert Church, Glendalough, Co. Wicklow*

example of Hiberno-Romanesque stone building in Ireland. It features a stone roof, fine ashlar walls with blind arcade decoration, an ordered chancel arch and south entrance, widespread use of geometrical patterning and some animal carving.

This fine ashlar work was not to last for long; thereafter, while quoins and openings continued to be well hewn, the bulk of the walls became rough-hewn, squared rubble or random, depending on the available local stone. Filling was rubble run with mortar. This type of wall construction was to be the dominant method employed in stone building for about seven centuries, until the economic boom of the seventeenth century.

Fig. 38 *Ashlar on Cormac's Chapel, Cashel, Co. Tipperary*

One of the most notable features of the Hiberno-Romanesque period was the tendency to treat important doorways and arches in a series of steps, or orders. This was facilitated by the great thickness of the walls. The west doorway of Clonfert Cathedral (Figure 39) in County Galway, for example, has eight distinct arches receding in the wall depth. These orders were sometimes retained as relatively

Fig. 39 *West doorway at Clonfert Cathedral, Co. Galway*

Fig. 40 *St MacDara's Island Church, Co. Galway*

simple steps, but were often expressed as highly decorative features. In the latter case, the carving included both geometrical patterns and animal or floral features, and these moved from stone to stone with a striking fluency. Each stone in these features had to be designed and carved individually, and often amounted to a conceptual jigsaw requiring both geometrical understanding and great creative skill.

Fig. 41 *Corbels at Reefert Church, Glendalough, Co. Wicklow*

Timber roofs were subject to both burning and biological deterioration, and a stone roof for these small churches was eventually developed. St MacDara's Island Church, County Galway (Figure 40) – at less than 6 metres long – is an elegant example. The wall containing the west (front) door was often framed between extended side walls in the form of antae, which seem to have been derived from the church's timber ancestors whose function was possibly decorative but also to support the gable roof overhang. In some churches, these antae also occurred on the east wall, and were common in timber-roofed stone churches. Later, they were replaced with corbels near roof level, which served equally well to support timber roof overhangs, as at Reefert Church (Figure 41) at Glendalough.[9]

There is some debate about the date of the relatively complex, corbelled, upside-down, boat-type of roof. Some see it as a directly evolving descendant of the *clocháns*, while many see it as a twelfth-century relative of the Irish vaulted stone roof but without the vault. There was a tendency for the side walls of these buildings to sag inwards, and many of these structures have collapsed. Gallarus Oratory in Dingle, County Kerry (Figure 42) is a very fine example and a success story. Here, the roof has only sagged a little, while about one mile away at Kilmalkedar, the remains of a collapsed oratory may be seen. Even the collapsed example seems to have lasted quite a long time, and its ultimate failure may have been due to foundation movement. The oratory at Gallarus is built on rock.

Fig. 42 *Gallarus Oratory, Dingle, Co. Kerry*

Fig. 43 *Vaulted stone roof*

As vertical side walls became higher, the inward-sagging tendency of the steeply sloping roof proved a problem. It is recorded that the side walls in the roof were supported by props until the apex stones were placed, but while the gables were fundamentally stable, the side walls were not, and sagging and collapses occurred. This problem was solved by the insertion of a propping arch, which gave rise to the vaulted stone roof, a strong element within the Irish building tradition. In many other countries, this type of vaulted construction was often covered by a timber roof with slates, as indeed it was in later work in Ireland.

The general concept of the Irish vaulted stone roof is shown in Figure 43 but in earlier examples the supporting arch is partially corbelled, a feature that O'Keeffe and Simington also note in various early bridges and which is illustrated in the bridge at Cadamstown in County Offaly (Figure 44). The walls of these stone-roofed churches were thick; in the tenth-century St Columba's House in Kells, for example, the walls were 1.2 metres thick. The plan size was 5.8 metres by 4.7 metres, the overall height 11.6 metres and the crown of the vault 7 metres above the floor. Champneys describes the roof construction process:

Fig. 44 *Medieval bridge, Cadamstown, Co. Offaly*

A centring of the required shape was made . . .
and was covered with wattles, giving the shape of
the arch required; on these a layer of mortar was
often put. Upon this temporary support more or
less wedge-shaped stones or merely flattish stones
– roughly shaped, perhaps, but not cut – were
laid edge downwards, lengthwise to the building,
smaller stones being inserted into the intervals,
where necessary, so as to jam these and give the
required radiation, though the sides were often . . .
merely corbelled out for some distance up, like a
'beehive' roof . . . Upon this vault thus formed half-
liquid mortar was poured until the gaps between
the stones were filled. If this mortar was good, as
it generally was, the result would be a sort of a
solid concrete arch . . . The sides were then filled
up so as to make a flat floor above; at the same
time, by thus weighing the sides of the vaulting,
its outward thrust was counteracted. In fact, such
barrel vaults exert very little thrust if the mortar is
good, the vault is more like a great rounded lintel
of concrete – many of the vaults so built in
Ireland are but slightly curved. Lastly the propping was removed, and the wattles broken or
burned away . . . Above such a vault as this the
high-pitched roof was built, the stones being
wrought to something like the proper shape and,
as a rule, simply laid one above another in mortar,

> like a piece of wall, not with slabs on the outside
> as in Cormac's Chapel; it was closed on the top on
> the inside with flags and the ridge of the roof was
> completed outside.[10]

In the particular case of Kells (built about 814) the roof was further strengthened by two cross walls, which were pierced by small doorways providing three rooms in the roof space.

Round Towers

The Irish name for a round tower is *cloigtheach*, or 'bell house'. Dating from the tenth to thirteenth centuries, they appear to be developments of the *cashel* and *clochán*. The first written reference to a bell tower is in 950 when the Four Masters record the burning by the Vikings of the belfry at Slane, County Meath, together with its occupants and their treasures. The latest record of the building of a round tower is in 1285, when the Annals of Innisfallen record the erection of the *cloigtheach* at Enachduin (Annadown) in County Galway. The round tower at Lusk in County Dublin (Figure 45) is a fine example of a tower incorporated into a later building. Towers are normally built of local stone; the one at Glendalough is built of local mica-schist with granite dressings around the windows and door. It is over 30 metres high and around 4.8 metres at the base.

In his book, *The Irish Round Tower*, Brian Lalor details 97 known towers, and identifies the stone used in 53 of them; Table 1 details this information:

Fig. 45 *Round tower, Lusk, Co. Dublin*

Table 1: *Stone used in 97 known round towers*

limestone	24
sandstone	14
granite	6
slate	3
basalt	2
mica-schist	1
shale	1
granite and limestone	1
rubble unclassified	1

The process of building a round tower began with a foundation trench or hole extending downwards to a bearing medium which satisfied the mason. In this, the substructure was constructed, generally using fairly rough stonework. The depth of substructure could be quite shallow where rock outcropped, but in some cases it exceeded 2 metres. At or near ground level, a flat surface was created and a firm centre point established to act as a reference point from which the building process was controlled by plumb line. The tower rose from this level in carefully controlled layers. External and internal faces were well built, and the space between filled with field stones set in mortar. The choice of random or ashlar face-work depended on the type of stone available and, we must suppose, the resources and wishes of the sponsor. Some show little dressing except around the openings. The towers generally decreased in external diameter as they rose. Internal floor timbers were sometimes supported on brackets or recesses, but more generally there was a change in the internal diameter at each floor level to accommodate the timber platform. The changing diameters, both inside and outside, meant that the mason had to be aware of the inner and outer diameter of each successive layer of stonework. Since the course heights were often variable, the top diameter of each course had to be accurately calculated to achieve the smooth batter that is so much a feature of the towers.

The earlier towers were fine examples of masonry without ornamentation. The development of the door and window heads from lintels through corbelled heads, curved lintels, false arches and ultimately true arches broadly followed the learning curve for the introduction of the circular arch in Irish building generally.[11] Some of the towers include decorative window and door opes in the Romanesque character, and some are of such a high quality that they constitute a status symbol for the establishment involved. The bells used in these towers – to summon the faithful or to give warning of danger – were hand bells of beaten iron of the order of 100–150 millimetres high; a few were of cast bronze based on the iron model, but up to 300 millimetres high.[12]

Transitional and Gothic

The Gothic style of architecture began to be seen in Ireland shortly after the arrival of the Cistercians, who came to Ireland with a mission to rectify the transgressions of the Irish clergy. In St Bernard of Clairvaux' *Life of St Malachy*, we learn of Malachy's horror as he travelled around Ireland:

Nowhere had he known such barbarism; nowhere had he found such moral obliquity, such deadly customs, such impiety, such savage laws, such stiffneckedness, such uncleanness of living; men Christian in name, pagan in fact.

The eight predecessors of Archbishop Cellach of Armagh, who ordained St Malachy, had been married laymen passing their inheritance on to family members through the exercise of tyrannical power. As Bishop of Armagh from 1132–36, Malachy sought the assistance of monks trained in Cistercian discipline to help in the revitalisation of the Irish Church. On a visit to Clairvaux, he left some of his monks to be trained in the order; when they were professed in the Rule of St Bernard, they returned to Ireland – together with a number of French monks – and established the first Cistercian monastery in 1142 at Mellifont, County Louth. The abbey – consecrated in 1157 – may have been designed by the monk Robert, an architect or master-builder from the Clairvaux house.

Twelve years later, in 1169, the Normans came to assist Dermott MacMurrough, King of Leinster. On his death in 1171, they inherited his kingdom. These events – Malachy's revitalisation of the Church and the arrival of the Normans – coincided with the effort of others and initiated a period of stone building that gave us monasteries, castles, keeps, cathedrals and other treasures in both the 'transitional' (that is, having elements of both Romanesque and Gothic) and the pure Gothic style. This caused a considerable upheaval in a country where permanence of abode was not especially desired and where mobility was valued. It appears that Irish timber-house structures were easily constructed and deconstructed, contributing to mobility, while stone was an unwelcome anchor. Power was reckoned in terms of people and livestock rather than property, and land and dwellings were moved to follow pastures. The practice of transhumance – moving between summer and winter pastures – was common down to relatively modern times.

> Certainly the Irish were contemptuous of the Anglo-Irish attachment to stone buildings. 'He was not engaged to keep stone walls,' MacMahon at the end of the twelfth century is reputed to have replied to the accusation of having abandoned his alliance with John de Courcy and destroyed his forts; 'he scorned to confine himself within such cold and dreary enclosures while the native woods were open for his reception and security.' Even in Church life, the showiness of the new Continental-inspired monasteries was ridiculed.[13]

The end of the twelfth and the entire thirteenth centuries saw the construction of a very large number of transitional and Gothic ecclesiastical buildings: 44 Cistercian foundations were established and, together with Franciscan,

Dominican, Augustinian, Carmelite and other minor establishments, brought the total to about 100. The discipline of the Cistercians demanded simplicity and avoidance of elaborate decoration in their buildings, yet many were quite sumptuous. *The Cistercian Monasteries of Ireland* by Roger Stalley gives a very detailed account of the important work of that order. He concludes that stone was mainly of local origin – giving the buildings a consistent character – though some stone from Dundry near Bristol was used in Dunbrody and Tintern, both in County Wexford, Graiguenamanagh and Jerpoint, both in County Kilkenny, St Mary's in Dublin, and Mellifont, County Louth; ease of access to navigable waters had been a deciding factor.

Stalley tells us that the masons were mainly laymen, with the monks supplying only advisory and supervisory support. Masons worked on different sites, and their marks can still be seen, though there is little knowledge of the particular work done by individuals. Building was generally slow due to lack of resources; Boyle, for example, took 60 years to complete, and Jerpoint about 50 years. Mellifont, on the other hand, took only fifteen years to complete. Many of the buildings began with greater architectural ambition than was ultimately achieved; at Corcomroe, famine and political unrest caused the quality of craftsmanship to decline significantly from excellent at the beginning to rudimentary at the end. The walls were normally of undressed masonry, with ashlar reserved for piers, shafts, arch mouldings and so on, but the standard of dressed work was high. When finished, the undressed walls were plastered, whitewashed and marked out with false ashlar. Roofs were usually covered with slates or tiles.

Planning of the monasteries was much more detailed than earlier Irish examples. Cistercian concepts of proportion and a certain ordering of buildings around a central covered-cloister garth gave the masons a model within which to work; an example is shown in Figure 46. There is little evidence of drawing, and the detail design existed only in the head of the master mason; thus, changes in style occur as masons changed, and setting-out errors resulting in misalignment often occurred.

The Synod of Kells in 1152 organised the Church into dioceses, and in the succeeding years these set about providing themselves with new cathedrals. Christ Church Cathedral in Dublin, begun by Archbishop John Comyn after his appointment in 1181, was completed about 1240, and

Fig. 46 *Layout of Mellifont Abbey, Co. Louth*

included the first pure Gothic work in Ireland in its nave and aisles. Much inspired by established English taste, it employed English craftsmen and used Dundry stone from England. St Patrick's, Dublin (Figure 47) – under construction from about 1220 to 1254 – was started as a collegiate church outside the city walls and was raised to the status of cathedral by Comyn's successor. Other cathedrals were built at Killaloe in County Clare, Newtown Trim in County Meath, Cashel in County Tipperary, Ardfert in County Galway (remodelled), Youghal and Cloyne, both in County Cork, Waterford, Limerick, Killala in County Mayo, Kilfenora in County Clare, Downpatrick in County Down, Ferns in County Wexford and Kilkenny. Large parish churches were also built; these include Cannistown in County Meath, St Doulagh's in Dublin's Raheny, New Ross, Kinsale, Youghal, Carrickfergus, County Antrim Killeigh in County Offaly, Drumcoo in County Galway, Kinlough in County Mayo, St Finghin's in Quinn, County Clare and Shanagolden in County Limerick. With about 100 monasteries, fifteen cathedrals, eleven large parish churches and other smaller churches under construction, the twelfth and thirteenth centuries was a boom time for the stone industry. When one considers that the Normans were also reinforcing their bridgeheads by surrounding themselves with stone and earthen strongholds, it must have stretched resources to the limit.

The story of the development from strongly Romanesque to pure Gothic is told most clearly in the detailing of the doors, windows, columns, arches and vaults, which display a riot of

Fig. 47 *Nave of St Patrick's, Dublin*

moulding and ornamentation. Some element of this development is apparent in a comparison between the door mouldings on the early twelfth-century Boyle Abbey with those of Graignamanagh Abbey, built in the thirteenth century. The abbey at Graignamanagh retains the Romanesque circular-door arch, but the mouldings are closer to those used in the Gothic features of Christ Church in Dublin.[14]

Town Walls

The practice of building protective walls around ecclesiastical sites was well established, and other small centres of population also had protective features, but this period saw the building of town walls on an unprecedented scale; at least 24 towns were encircled in stone by the end of the thirteenth century. The walls incorporated towers, gates and gatehouses, which in some cases were quite substantial. Figure 48 shows one of the still-intact town gates at the fortified twelfth-century abbey in Fore, County Westmeath.

Fig. 48 *Gate to the abbey town of Fore, Co. Westmeath*

Cork had 1.6 kilometres of wall up to 4.5 metres thick, fourteen towers of various shapes and sizes, and three main gates incorporating four-storeyed gatehouse structures, as well as a number of water gates. Construction or improvement of town walls was financed by the garrison, by the burghers or by 'murage' (walling) grants or charges, which could be raised in a number of ways, such as tolls on traders, import charges on wine or relief from taxes. The protection of Cork with stone walls seems to have started around 1210, but the first record of a murage grant is in 1284 when a charter established a five-year grant for murage and pontage (bridge works).[15]

Castles

Before the Normans, there were seven sites in which castles are mentioned, but they were probably not of stone. It was not long after the Normans established themselves that the Gaelic lords began to emulate them, and during the twelfth and thirteenth centuries, at least 26 castles/keeps were constructed.

The major military castles – such as Carrickfergus, Trim, and Carlow (Figure 49) – all originate from this time. Many had extensive outer protective walling around a bawn – a fortified enclosure – in which animals and other property could be secured behind strong gateways in the masonry. Carlow Castle had a rectangular plan with circular turrets at each corner; the turrets were 4.5 metres in internal diameter and the walls were just under 3 metres thick. The finest of the circular castles is the Butler stronghold at Nenagh, County

Fig. 49 *Remains of the towered castle at Carlow*

Tipperary. It is largely intact, though the subject of some alterations and reconstruction. Almost 17 metres in diameter, it was originally 23 metres high; its lowest walls are almost 6 metres thick, reducing to 3.3 metres thick at the top.

These castles now seem romantic and picturesque, but originally they were serious defensive structures with walls generally of the order of 3–6 metres thick. The materials for their construction were largely local, with stone quarried from the moats being used until it ran out. Well-wrought sandstone dressings were used for the surrounds of windows and doors through the twelfth and early thirteenth centuries, and limestone dressings were also used thereafter. Many of these structures feature again in the succeeding centuries as reconstruction, renovation and expansion projects.

There was so much work going on in this period that one can reasonably assume that much of it was done by locally trained people working under the general direction of qualified masons. Quarry-men, transporters, lime burners and general labourers recruited both locally and from the military would have served a smaller number of qualified stone workers. In this way, operations would have been speeded up.

5

Black Death & Cannons

Historical Context

The fourteenth century was a traumatic period, with the Bruce invasion of 1315 and the Black Death of 1348 halving the population from a high of about 750,000. The growth of the previous epoch was succeeded by a period of degeneration. Nevertheless, this period sees the first mention of a stone bridge; according to the Four Masters, it was built across the river of Eas Dara in 1362.[1]

Town Walls and Paving

The practice of protecting towns with stone walls continued, with at least another fourteen new sites demanding the attention of stoneworkers in the fourteenth century, five in the fifteenth and seven in the sixteenth century. Figure 50 shows parts of the extant walls around Waterford, while Figure 51 show St Lawrence's Gate in the old walls of Drogheda. Many of the earlier walls required improvement or repair, and murage facilities were again granted. In a charter of 1333 for Kinsale, the town was said to be 'surrounded by Irish enemies

Fig. 50 *Waterford's walls*

and English rebels . . . the walls are ruinous and the burgesses not able to repair them'.[2] The battlemented stone walls of Dungarvan – constructed in the late fifteenth century with the aid of murage tolls – were almost 1 kilometre long, and had four corner towers, two main gates and a water gate.

The paving of streets was undertaken in important centres around this time. Paving can entail some simple surface dressing or may entail dressing with natural stone or cut stone. Whatever the scale, Dublin city fathers put monies aside for the completion of the paving in 1336, and in 1586 it was proposed that everyone should pave the area in front of their own door. In 1681, as a result of poor service from untrained paviers, it was resolved that

> the said paviers be and are hereby added as a wing
> unto the masons, and that noe person be for the

future admitted to make any pavements but such
who shall be soe incorporated, their apprentices
or servants.[3]

Cut-stone paving was particularly favoured in the
Georgian period, and the stone industry supplied paving

Fig. 51 *St Lawrence's Gate, Drogheda*

slabs, setts and kerbs right up to the twentieth century, when other forms of paving became more popular or economical. Stone continues to be used, with other materials, to surface some pavements and pedestrian areas in cities and towns.

Ecclesiastical Building

While no monasteries were built in the fourteenth century, there was a further influx of Franciscan, Dominican, Carmelite, Augustinian and other minor orders of friars. Though most of their buildings were of small scale, they were numerous. Maurice Craig in *The Architecture of Ireland from Earliest Times to 1880* provides details:

> The same period (1349–1539) saw the building of sixty new mendicant houses, plus a further forty-four of the third order or 'tertiaries' who lived under a less strict rule . . . there are remains or ruins of some interest of thirty-six Franciscan houses, twenty-nine Dominican, sixteen Augustinian, fifteen nunneries of various kinds, thirteen Carmelite, and twenty-one of the Franciscan Third Order; a grand total of one hundred and thirty, not counting oddments such as the Trinitarians at Adare or the Fratres Cruciferi at Newtown Trim.[4]

Only a few can be assigned to the fourteenth century, among them Athenry, Castledermot, the Dominican 'Black Abbey' of Kilkenny, and Adare, an Augustinian house modified in the fifteenth and nineteenth centuries.

An interesting and innovative feature of the friaries, from the point of view of stonework, was their towers, and with many buildings this is the only feature to have survived. Most of these towers were added some time after the main friary was built. The friary of the Friars Minor at Castledermot in County Carlow (Figure 52) was built in the early fourteenth century; though it does not have a tower, it has other fine features, such as doors, windows and internal arches in dressed granite. The friary of the Franciscans at Moyne in County Mayo (Figure 53) is a fifteenth-century foundation whose tower and general building layout has survived. A peculiarly well-endowed establishment, it has a full set of buildings arranged around a vaulted ambulatory and cloister garth. The Magdalene tower of the Dominican Friary in Drogheda – an addition to the original building – is carried on thick walls,

Fig. 52 *Castledermot Friary, Co. Carlow*

Fig. 53 *Franciscan Friary, Moyne, Co. Mayo*

or piers, independent of the existing church walls. It was located so as to separate the choir and the nave, which thereafter were accessed through the high pointed archway. Thought to be of the early fourteenth century, this would make it one of the first stone belfries added to an Irish friary.

An important development in stonework attributable to the early fourteenth century is the use of multiple stone-mullioned windows with embellishments, commonly called 'switch-line tracery'. In its simplest form, this involves two lancet windows with the central mullion curving to left and right to form pointed tops and a lozenge-shape top light. This occurred in many friaries and developed to include three, four and five-light windows, with tracery of geometrical complexity beautifully carved in stone. Figure 54 shows the switch-line tracery of the east window in Clontuskert Abbey, County Galway.

While there was no significant work on the monasteries in
the fourteenth century, many of the cloisters were rebuilt in

Fig. 54 *East window in Clontuskert Abbey, Co. Galway*

Fig. 55 *Cloister ambulatory at Ballintober Abbey, Co. Mayo*

the fifteenth century. Figure 55 shows the general layout of a typical covered-cloister ambulatory at Ballintober, County. Mayo. The treatment of the cloister walls was an opportunity for considerable flourishes in stone; the plain piers became columns of more complex cross section, often of dumbbell shape appearing as two small columns connected integrally. Often ornately decorated, the masons' enjoyment of this fine work is evidenced by a great number of mason's marks denoting 'ownership'. Figure 56 is an example of columns that are of round section. Other cross sections occurred, such as octagonal or hexagonal, and some were twisted along their length. The Cistercian cloister garth became both a tranquil, covered ambulatory and an artistic delight far removed from the austerity and absence of decoration intended by the founding fathers.

Fig. 56 *Cloister column at Jerpoint Abbey, Co. Kilkenny*

As the Anglo-Norman and Gaelic nobility were fond of establishing or supporting religious houses in their territory, there was both an aggrandisement of fabric and a superfluity of such establishments, and it was not long before there was squabbling among the abbeys and friaries over principles, lands and resources. The monasteries were dissolved in 1536–43, and although this impacted on the stone industry, it was not a catastrophic event as much of the building work was completed in advance and stone workers were deployed elsewhere. It was, however, significant in marking the cessation of fine-detailed carving for a long time.

Tower Houses

There seems to have been little castle building in the fourteenth century; some begun in the last part of the previous century were completed in the early part of the fourteenth century, but all major work appears to have ceased by about 1320, following the Bruce invasion. An important, new phase of building got underway around 1430, in the form of tower houses designed to secure the nobles.[5] These were vertical buildings in which rooms were stacked on top of one another. The walls were thick and battered, and there was usually a talus, or base batter, at ground level. Figure 57 shows a late-fifteenth-century tower. From the point of view of stone building, there is nothing exceptional about these towers houses; they were generally of local stone with only limited use of dressed stone. The quality of the stonework and the similarities with the friary towers leads some authorities to assert that the same masons were sometimes responsible for both types of structure. Most of the early examples were without fireplaces or chimneys; later, when these were installed, masons often took the opportunity to show off their carving, and sometimes included the initials of the owner and his wife, and perhaps the mason's own.[6]

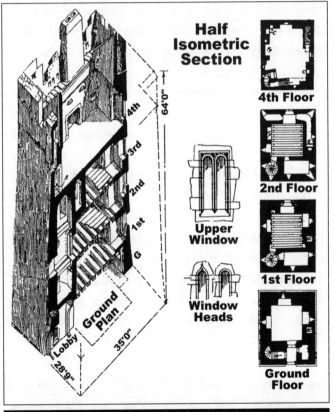

Fig. 57 *Clara Castle, Co. Kilkenny*[7]

Of the estimated 2,900 castles or keeps suggested by Leask,[8] only seven per cent were within the Pale. In an effort to secure the planted territories, the Dublin parliament in 1429 authorised the subsidising of castle building in Dublin, Meath, Kildare and Louth to the tune of £10, providing the structures were of sufficient strength and at least 20 feet by 16 feet by 40 feet high; in 1449, this was altered to 15 feet by 12 feet by 40 feet, and numbers were limited. Many of the minor castles around Dublin, such as Pucks and Kilgobbin, could be counted among these £10 castles.

Gunpowder and Low-level Fortification

By the mid-fourteenth century, most main towns had protective walls or protective earthworks, but both these and the masonry castles and towers became largely ineffective when cannon was introduced. The first use of artillery in siege warfare occurred in 1453, when the Turks took Constantinople. Subsequent deployment in European wars led to the development of low-level fortifications, notably in Italy and Holland. At this time, the governance of Ireland was in the hands of a combination of Anglo-Norman and Gaelic nobles. Garret Mór Fitzgerald, the eighth Earl of Kildare, was the first to use cannon for siege work in Ireland when, in 1488, he set up two guns 140 yards from the Mac Geoghan stronghold at Balrath Castle, County Westmeath and substantially ruined the building.[9] The king's deputy, he used the early ordnance pieces to help secure his own interests as well as those of the king. From this time onwards, it was necessary to think in terms of anti-artillery fortifications, and castles and keeps which lacked these could only be relied on to provide security from attackers using small arms. When faced with cannon, they were doomed, and in many cases the occupants had no option but to surrender. The English Crown eventually had to dislodge the Irish nobles. In 1535, Sir William Skeffington took Kildare's castle at Maynooth, and thereafter Lord Deputy Grey took control of the other castles of the Butlers and the Fitzgeralds, and tried to rule Ireland from Dublin.

In 1551 and 1602 respectively, the English engineers, John Rodgers and Paul Ive, planned and supervised fortification works at Cork and Kinsale in line with the new needs for security from cannon. Fortifications involved the provision of suitable stands from which to fire at attackers, together with configurations that provided for horizontal strafing of anyone attempting to rush the walls. Low walls protecting the gun stands and projections from which the defenders could fire along the walls were the basic solution.

With growing political stability and an expanding population, work in stone was included in some infrastructural works, such as bridges and small stone buildings for mills. A sign that some people were looking forward to greater tranquillity was the development of big-house-type semi-fortified castles, the first being Ormond Manor House at Carrick-on-Suir (Figure 58) in the 1560s. Another was built at Rathfarnham around 1590 by Sir Adam Loftus, and the following century saw a continuation of this trend.

Fig. 58 *Ormond Manor House, Carrick-on-Suir, Co. Tipperary*

Introduction of Clay Brickwork

The formerly unassailable position of stone as the basic building material was beginning to alter as brickwork came on the
scene. Bricks were mentioned as commodities liable for
murage duty as far back as 1283,[10] though it is not known if
they were imported; their precise function at this time is also
not clear. Amongst the earliest recorded use of brick in building was in the vaulting in one of the towers of Bunratty
Castle, which was completed around 1467. Bricks were also
used in parts of Ormond Manor House and in Carrickfergus
Castle, where local bricks featured around the windows; the
rest of the castle was built of local dolerite and basalt, with
quoins of magnesian limestone shipped across Belfast Lough
from Cultra, County Down.

6

Exit Earls, Enter Georgiana

Historical Context

In the closing years of the sixteenth century, Crown forces were constructing strong points in the northern part of the country with a view to dislodging the Earl of Tyrone, Hugh O'Neill, who was hanging on tenaciously. Gun embrasures had been constructed at Carrickfergus as early as 1561–67 even though its town walls were not yet completed in 1596. The south of the country was more or less secured by the English after the Battle of Kinsale in 1601, and the Crown turned its full attention to Ulster. The O'Neill strongholds were taken, including the castle of Dungannon, and new forts were constructed. O'Neill surrendered in 1603, and the 'Flight of the Earls' took place in 1607.

Forts and Military Engineers

By this time, the crown had a network of strategically located forts throughout the north, with Dutch and English engineers having assisted in the design of some of them. Thereafter, the Crown consolidated its hold, building new forts and strengthening others. The temporary campaign forts at Derry were replaced during 1614–18 with masonry defences of ramparts and bastions, planned with the advice of Captain Panton, a military engineer.[1] The city of London was responsible for the plantation around Derry; it supplied the finances necessary for its fortification and caused its name to be changed to Londonderry. A 1618–19 report to London reported that

> The city of Londonderry is now encompassed
> with a very strong wall, excellently made and
> neatly wrought, being all of good lime and stone
> . . . in every place of it the wall is 24ft high and 6ft
> thick and backed with 12ft of earth.[2]

Other towns to be walled in the seventeenth century included Coleraine, County Derry (1610–12), Bandon, County Cork (1620–27) and Belfast (1642), although the latter was mainly an earthen rampart with a ditch together with stone-reinforced gates and bastions.

Throughout Europe, military engineers were playing an important role in the design and construction of fortifications. Officers in the Swedish army were formed into the first corps of engineers in 1641, while other European armies followed suit in the remaining years of the seventeenth century. Such engineers, many of them with Continental experience,[3] managed the provision and improvement of artillery and defence fortifications for both sides during the Cromwellian

Wars, which ended in 1652. Later, fear of a Spanish or French attack caused the military to undertake protection of the shore from naval attack, and a number of substantial batteries were constructed. These included works at the head of Bantry Bay, at the entrance to Berehaven and at Rosscarbery, all in County Cork. The great Charles Fort in Kinsale, County Cork (Figure 59) was constructed during 1678–80, and was considered a masterpiece. Its fatal flaw became apparent when it was taken during the Jacobite war in 1690: overlooked by higher ground, it gave the advantage to the attacker. Incidentally, there were French and Neapolitan engineers with the Jacobite army in Ireland between 1689–91.[4]

Whilst London suffered its great fire in 1666, there was

Fig. 59 *Charles Fort, Kinsale, Co. Cork*

no shortage of fires in the various towns of Ireland; in 1622, about 1,500 houses were lost in the great fire of Cork. Although it may be fanciful to make too much of this event in terms of its influence on the choice of future building materials, it is clear that we have, today, a greater number of surviving buildings, made largely of stone, whose foundations post-date that event. The London inferno certainly had a deep influence on many of the architects and engineers who came here to work for the English establishment. Sir William Robinson, surveyor general from 1671–1700, designed Charles Fort, and there is considerable information about the organisation of the contract for the building. Five officers were nominated to oversee the work, and contracts were entered into with local 'artificers and others building the works'. Rates of pay for a day's work were agreed. The work started with a 'beat of drum' at five in the morning and ended with another beat of drum at seven in the evening; subtracting time for the agreed three breaks, workers put in twelve hours of labour. The contractors were to provide all materials and workmen, including masons, quarry-men and labourers. The walls were of squared rubble and the angles – or quoins of the ramparts – bastions, gun embrasures and sally points were to be built of hewn stone or ashlars.[5] The quality of the work is well attested by the continuing survival of the walls with little maintenance.

Robinson also did work for Dublin Castle, where he introduced a new style of arcading involving eleven bays of columns and arches, giving a covered ambulatory at ground-floor level.

The construction and maintenance of fortifications lapsed in the comparative peace of the eighteenth century, and it was not until the rebellion of 1798 and the threat of Napoleonic invasion that further significant stone-fortification work was

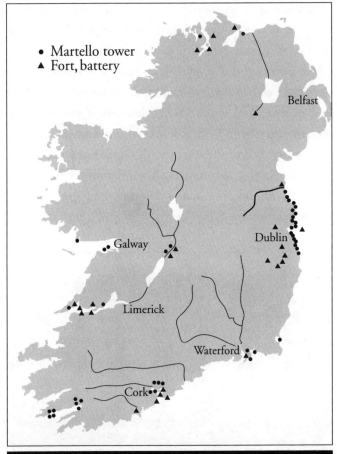

Fig. 60 *Forts, batteries and Martello towers, 1793–1813*[6]

undertaken. Figure 60 shows the extent of forts, batteries and Martello towers that were renewed, built or extended between 1793–1813.

Semi-fortified Castles

The building of castles and semi-fortified buildings as status symbols became an established trend despite their unsuitability as serious defensive structures. The main fabric of these buildings was rough stone, but there was some fine wrought work in doorways, windows, sally ports, fireplaces and quoins. MacDonagh MacCarthy built a fine castle/house at Kanturk, County Cork around 1609, and others were built in the first half of the seventeenth century at Portumna in County Galway (Figure 61), Manorhamilton in County Leitrim, Raphoe in County Donegal and Burncourt in County Tipperary . These were generally of rectangular plan,

Fig. 61 *Portumna Castle, Co. Galway*

Fig. 62 *Drimnagh Castle, Co. Dublin*

with 'flanker' towers on each corner. Drimnagh Castle in County Dublin (Figure 62) was modified for more comfortable living, and Eyrecourt in County Galway and Carton in County Kildare are further examples of the trend towards semi-fortified accommodation. Slane Castle, in County Meath, was built around 1786 as a country house for a surviving Catholic planter family, and it is suggested that its castellated features may have more to do with an effort to establish the impression of long-term ownership than with defensive needs.[7]

Family aggrandisement often lies behind the construction of stone follies built by landed families about and since this time. Figure 63 shows such a structure. Known as the

Fig. 63 *The Jealous Wall, Mullingar, Co. Westmeath*

Jealous Wall and located in the grounds of Belvedere House near Mullingar, it was built by Lord Belfield as a Gothic pseudo-ruin in the mid-eighteenth century so as to increase the apparent age of his estate and also to spoil the view from the neighbouring Tudenham House of which he was jealous. Follies were also built to provide employment in times of need. Connolly's Folly at Castletown, for example, was built in 1741 after a severe frost caused a short famine.

Public and Ecclesiastical Building

Sir William Robinson's successor as surveyor general was Thomas Burgh, a man who left a very significant legacy of fine stone buildings, including the Royal Barracks, Dublin (1701, now Collins Barracks) the Library at Trinity College, Dublin (1732), St Werburgh's Church, Dublin (1715) and

Dr Steeven's Hospital, Dublin (1718). In these, we see a return to fine ashlar work and a revived appreciation of the value of attention to detail in façade stonework, which lapsed in the medieval era. The office of surveyor general seems to have declined around 1760, when a 'Barrack Board' was established; it was composed of notables who had common cause with the Crown.

Some Church of Ireland building was taking place in the early seventeenth century, such as Kilbrogan near Bandon (1610), Derrygonnelly, County Fermanagh (1623) and the cathedral at Derry (1628). The benefits of peace were beginning to show in Dublin, too, with the building of Trinity College (1630s), the Tholsel (town hall, 1676) and the King's Hospital School (1680). The great project to house the veteran soldiers at the Royal Hospital Kilmainham commenced in 1680, and provided the blueprint for its successor at Chelsea, commenced in 1682. These buildings illustrate the classical building revival taking place in and around Dublin at this time, with attention to detail its hallmark.

The capital began to establish itself as the second city of the empire in the eighteenth century with such stone masterpieces as the Royal Barracks (1701, now Collins Barracks), Dr Steeven's Hospital (1718), Castletown (1722), Linen Hall (1728), Rotunda (1749), Trinity West Front (1752), Casino (1759), Genealogical Office (1763), City Hall (1769), Trinity Examination Hall and Chapel (1775), Custom House (1782), Blue Coat School (1783), Four Courts (1786) and King's Inns (1795–1817). Figure 64 shows the Casino,

Fig. 64 *Casino, Marino, Dublin*

designed by Sir William Chambers and built on Lord Charlemont's lands at Marino, while Figure 65 shows some of the detail of the stonework. These fine projects tell of a building industry which was very productive and which

Fig. 65 *Casino (detail)*

needed additional resources from overseas to achieve its output. In the building of Gandon's Custom House, for example, stonecutters and stonemasons were brought in from England to supplement the local craftsmen.

Engineers, acknowledging the importance of stone in the provision of fine buildings and bridges, paid attention to the technological developments within the industry during the mid-eighteenth century. In 1766, a military engineer published a book aimed at assisting in the determination of the sizes and shapes of each stone in curved work, including complex splayed arches (C. Vallancy, *A Practical Treatise on Stonecutting*),[8] and in 1776, another engineer and builder produced a seminal work on the problems of building in water (George Semple, *A Treatise on Building in Water*),[9] including valuable advice on the selection and use of lime mortars in such situations.

Although stonework was still prominent in major building works, the use of brickwork was expanding. Jigginstown House (1634) near Naas in County Kildare (Figure 66) is the oldest Irish building constructed entirely of brick. The bricks were made locally and not imported from Belgium as is sometimes asserted, though it was not until the next century that substantial quantities of brick were manufactured for use in this country.

Significant public monies were granted for the development of public, and indeed private, works after about 1750, and these contributed to the growth of a strong building industry. The efficiency of the application of these funds

Fig. 66 *Jigginstown House, Co. Kildare*

remains a matter for debate, but it certainly seems that the
'brothers of the Ascendancy' who made up the Barracks
Board, the grand juries and other bodies charged with development were not immune or averse to improper influence.
Various efforts to ensure value for public monies led to the
formation of the Commissioners of Public Works in the following century.

Many of the fine stone courthouses, market houses or
assembly houses still in use today were constructed in the
eighteenth century, among them those at Kinsale, County
Cork (1706), Antrim (1726), Dunlavin, County Wicklow
(1743), Lifford, County Donegal (1746), Loughgall, County
Armagh (1746), Portaferry, County Down (1752),
Castlewellan, County Down (1764), Newtownards, County

Down (1765) and Belfast (1769). A neat example exists at Blessington, County Wicklow (Figure 67), where the ground-level arcading has been filled in during restoration as an office for the local Credit Union. The market-house function led to arcaded street levels; a particularly good example, designed by Fernando Stratford, a canal engineer from Bristol, is at Newtownards, County Down. In Belfast, the prosperity of the linen industry was illustrated by the commencement in 1754 of the Brown Linen Hall and of the White Linen Hall in 1784, both of which established Belfast as the chief centre for the buying and selling of fabrics, and which effectively bypassed the Dublin Linen Hall.

The vibrant building industry of this time was a product

Fig. 67 *Courthouse, Blessington, Co. Wicklow*

of economic growth; livestock, milling, warehousing and transport were key to the commercial success of this period.

Mills

There were a number of windmills in use in Ireland from the seventeenth century onwards, such as those at St Columb's College in Derry (1688–89) and at Ballycopeland, County Down (1784). Windmill towers are usually conical and composed of rubble, with only a little dressed work; water mills are more widespread and more significant from the point of view of stonework. Legal tracts show that water mills were used in the seventh and eighth centuries, and their use was extensive in the manorial system of Anglo-Norman medieval Ireland; a 1654 civil survey found substantial numbers of mills in those counties surveyed. Seventeenth and early-eighteenth-century water mills were very small – normally two storeys – and were often ineffective during periods of dry weather. Their purpose was to grind produce for local use, with bakers themselves undertaking sifting and refining in the bakeries. Only small quantities were sold beyond the immediate neighbourhood.

In 1758, a policy of paying bounties to subsidise transport costs – often greater than the actual transport costs – was introduced to assist in supplying grain and flour to the Dublin market, thus increasing the profitability of milling. New water-powered mills were constructed to provide services such as sifting and shelling before grinding, and which provided the bakers with cleaner flour. Drying facilities and large storage areas were also a feature of these mills, thus ensuring uninterrupted supplies to city markets.[10] The first 'modern' mill was built at Naul, County Meath around 1761. By 1762, mills in Counties Meath, Westmeath, Kilkenny, Limerick, Carlow, King's County (now Offaly), Queen's County (now Laois) and Tipperary were consigning large quantities of flour to Dublin.

An estimated 248 mills were built between 1758–90 to supply the Dublin market, the most impressive being a complex of three structures built on the River Barrow between 1786–90 at Milford, County Carlow (Figure 68). These were

Fig. 68 *Millford Mill, Co. Carlow*

38.1 metres by 13.7 metres, with six storeys. Twenty-two pairs of millstones worked continuously, while a single wheel drove thirteen of them, with all their attendant machinery.

As textile mills became common around 1770, a number of flour mills were adapted for cotton milling. In 1783, Balbriggan in north County Dublin had a five-storey-high cotton mill measuring 30.5 metres by 10.4 metres. The first water-powered scutch mill was set up near Belfast around 1740; eventually, they were widespread, particularly in Ulster. Typically, these buildings were small, single-storey or two-storey buildings with rubble walling. In 1766, the first really large mill was built at Slane; at 42 metres long, the cut-stone building was the largest industrial structure in the country, exceeded in scale only by such buildings as the Royal Hospital. Much of its cost related to massive waterworks, such as the great weir, retaining walls and floodgates through which lighters could travel in order to bring produce to Drogheda via the Boyne and Boyne Navigation. Arthur Young, in his *Tour of Ireland 1776–9*, describes operations at the mill in Slane:

> The corn upon being unloaded is hoisted through
> doors in the floors to the upper storey of the
> building, by a very simple contrivance, being
> worked by the water wheel, and discharged into
> spacious granaries which hold 5,000 barrels. From
> thence it is conveyed, during 7 months of the year,
> to the kiln for drying, the mill containing two,

IRELAND—INDUSTRIAL AND COMMERCIAL.
(As seen by Arthur Young in 1776-9.)

Fig. 69 *Arthur Young's industrial landscape of Ireland*[12]

which will dry 80 barrels in 24 hours. From the
kiln it is hoisted again to the upper storey, from
thence to a fanning machine for redressing, to get

out dirt, soil, etc. And from thence, by a small
sifting machine, into the hoppers, to be ground,
and is again hoisted into the bolting mills, to be
dressed into flour, different sorts of pollard and
bran. In all which progress, the machinery is con-
trived to do the business with the least labour
possible . . .[11]

Young's impression of the industrial landscape (Figure 69)
illustrates the significance of linen and milling to Ireland's
economy, though at this stage linen was mainly produced as
a farm-based product.

Milling gave rise to a greater need for warehouses, and

Fig. 70 *Corn store at Leighlin Bridge, Co. Carlow*

some of these were of significant size. The Corn Store at Leighlin Bridge, County Carlow (Figure 70) – a fine example – is still substantially intact, and efforts to remodel it are progressing. Many mills, their ancillary buildings and their watercourses were built of stone, but some brick was also used.

Ports

Transport to and from Ireland and within the island itself depended on the ports, and the development of vital port infrastructure was a strong feature of stone building in the eighteenth century. Stonework executed in Dublin Port to enhance harbour and warehousing facilities will serve to illustrate this important aspect of building (while acknowledging that similar facilities were being developed at many other ports). Dublin was a busy port in the eighteenth century, although it was not suitable for vessels of deep draft; Dalkey Sound was used as an anchorage where cargoes were transferred to and from smaller boats or partially discharged before ships could enter Dublin Port. Equipped with wooden quay walls and slips, a grant in 1560 allowed for the provision of stonework to keep the slips and walls stiff and strong, and in 1620, a lease was granted for the building of a custom house and wharf intended to be the only proper place for loading and discharging ships. Three custom houses were built in succession, each proving in time to be inadequate for its purpose. The present Custom House (Figure 71), built in 1791, was designed by James Gandon, an Englishman who met opposition in Dublin but who is held by many to be the greatest of the architects to have practiced here

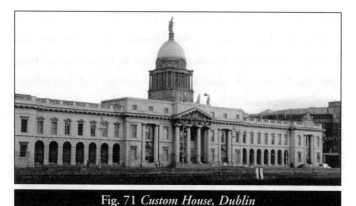

Fig. 71 *Custom House, Dublin*

in the eighteenth century. The stonework in the Custom House is a masterpiece of the mason's work.

Bridges

Stone has been used as a bridge-building material in Dublin since about the fifteenth century, but many of the bridges date from the seventeenth and eighteenth centuries. Figure 72 shows the fine quality of detailing in the elevation of the central arch of Essex (now Grattan) Bridge, as illustrated in George Semple's eighteenth-century *Treatise on Building in Water*[13] in which the rebuilding in 1755 of the earlier collapsed bridge is described. At this time, ships came up as far as Essex Bridge, and the old Custom House was just downstream.

Quays and Docks

Efforts to improve the navigability of the Liffey included the building of the Great South Wall and the Poolbeg lighthouse

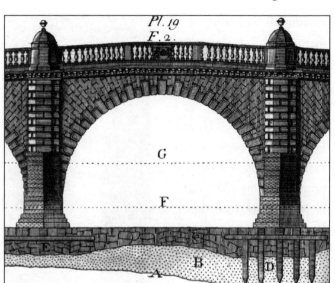

Fig. 72 *Essex Bridge, Dublin*

in 1767.[14] Straightening and deepening of the channel started around 1711. The building of the stone retaining walls, which contain the Liffey as it is now, seems to have been started about 1717, and to have provided work for the stone industry on and off from then until the early twentieth century. A stone wall measuring 914 metres, from Sir John Rogerson's Quay to the mouth of the River Dodder, was built between 1717–27, and while timber caissons were used in the early works on the Great South Wall, the stone version was completed in 1796 using large, granite blocks from the Dublin Mountains and rubble from Bullock and Clontarf. An indication of the scale of construction is illustrated by the 2,000 mountain stones, measuring between 1.5 metres and 2.1 metres in length, that Lord Ranelagh supplied to the Ballast Office in 1779.

The Custom House Dock, which opened in 1796, was very large for its time, measuring 135 metres by 60.4 metres. Its designer was John Rennie, in response to a brief from James Gandon.[15] There were two John Rennies – father and son – and both were involved in Dublin port.

The Grand Canal Dock was built near Ringsend between 1792–96. In two sections and spread over 10 hectares, it provided 1,615 metres of wharfage. The dock, together with its attendant three tidal locks, represented a huge project for which the contractor, John Macartney, was knighted.[16]

Fig. 73 *Fastnet lighthouse*

Lighthouses

There are many fine examples around Ireland of stone lighthouse towers. John Smeaton's magnificent Eddystone lighthouse, off Plymouth, was completed in 1759. Interlocking blocks of stone were a feature of Smeaton's work, and others adopted his technique, among them George Halpin, Senr., designer of the Fastnet Rock lighthouse (Figure 73). Figure 74 shows how this dovetailing was achieved in the top courses of the tower, which are seen here in a dry assembly at the manufacturer's yard before being shipped to site.

Work on the Fastnet commenced in 1896:

> The tower is built of Cornish granite . . . each of
> the granite blocks being dovetailed into adjacent

Fig. 74 *Fastnet lighthouse top, assembled dry at Penrhyn, Wales*

blocks in each ring of masonry. The tower contains 58,000 cu. ft of masonry weighing 4,300 tons, each of the 2,074 blocks being placed by hand . . . The base diameter of the tower is 52 ft tapering to 40 ft at a height of 20 ft above the base . . . the total height of the masonry tower is 179 ft 6 inches.[17]

Inland Navigation

Transporting produce to the towns and cities was very difficult prior to the construction of canals and railways. The first Act of Parliament relating to inland navigation, passed in 1715, proved ineffective due to the inability of local interests to provide necessary capital and technical skills. A 1729 Act of Parliament established the Commissioners of Inland Navigation for Ireland to control inland navigation in Ireland.

Edward Lovett Pearce, later surveyor general, had been joined in his practice in 1728 by a younger architect and engineer, Richard Castle, who was to play an important part in the successful implementation of the proposals. A manuscript by Castle entitled 'An Essay on Artificial Navigation' – now lodged in the National Library of Ireland – deals with fluid behaviour, canal engineering and basic mathematical physics. As surveyor general, Pearce was directly responsible for implementing many of the suggestions and proposals contained in the Act of Parliament, but following his death in 1733, Richard Castle took complete control of the Newry Navigation from 1734–36, and was probably the first person to build a stone lock chamber in Ireland. The English engineer, Thomas Steers – then building a new dock at Liverpool – replaced Castle upon Castle's dismissal, and oversaw the work up to its opening in 1742, when the first collier, the *Cope,* arrived in Dublin with Tyrone coal.

The Lagan Navigation was begun in 1733 and the Tyrone Navigation in 1756. The Lagan Navigation Aqueduct at Goatum took three years to build; begun in 1783, it was constructed with

> the most excellent stone of the Earl of Hillsborough at Kilwarlin quarried some two miles from the site. Between Aghalee and Lough Neagh there were ten large locks each 70ft x 16ft over a distance of 3.25 miles.[18]

These canals involved stone quay walls and locks whose walls and sills were precisely wrought and constructed. Their construction established canal-building capabilities that extended into the next century, and a core of engineers and skilled craftsmen whose expertise contributed substantially to the quality of subsequent stone buildings.

Work on the Barrow Navigation continued throughout the eighteenth century. Figure 75 illustrates the convenience of canals – the mill at Levitstown between Carlow and Athy is sited close to the Barrow Navigation lock – while Figure 76 shows the Huband Aqueduct on the Grand Canal near

Tullamore in County Offaly, where the occupants of Ballycowan Castle had easy access.

Canal works also provided the stone industry with projects in the Dublin region. The Grand Canal began at the basin in James' Street and headed first to Sallins in County Kildare. This section was opened in 1779, and the canal did not reach the Shannon until 1804. The final section of the

Fig. 75 *Levitstown Lock, Co. Kildare*

Fig. 76 *Huband Aqueduct, Co. Offaly*

Grand Canal – linking the basin at James' Street with the Liffey near Ringsend – was completed in 1796. Stone workers were employed in the construction of the five aqueducts, two dry docks, 30 single locks and six double locks. The largest aqueduct is near Sallins, where it carries the canal over the Liffey.[19] The overall length of this fine limestone ashlar structure is 71 metres, its width 14 metres. It has five 7.6-metre span arches, a towpath, roadway and a 5-metre-wide waterway.

Work on the Royal Canal got underway in 1790 and took 27 years to complete. Interesting stonework along its route

Fig. 77 *Royal Canal Aqueduct over River Inny, Co. Longford*

includes a 70-metre-long tunnel with a semicircular arched stone roof of 9.1 metres width, two major aqueducts, 36 single locks, ten double locks and a dry dock at Richmond Harbour. Figure 77 shows the Royal Canal Aqueduct, which carries the canal across the River Inny near the Longford–Westmeath border.

Interesting stonework features at other canals, including the Barrow branch of the Grand Canal from Lowtown to Athy in County Kildare, the Eglington and Cong Canal in County Galway, the Jamestown Canal near Drumsna in County Leitrim, the Limerick and Killaloe Navigation from Killlaloe in County Clare to the mouth of the River Abbey in Limerick, and the Tralee–Blennerville Canal in County Kerry.

7

Famine, Science &
Commerce

Famine

The nineteenth century was one of contrast and achievement in an Ireland overshadowed by famine. This period of death and distress led to a decline in population from 8.1 million to 6.5 million in three years. The official response to the Famine has been criticised – food was needed, not work. Yet by March 1847, over 700,000 people were employed on relief schemes under the control of the Board of Works. Supervisory staff numbered 14,000, including more than 76 inspecting officers – all military men – and 500 engineers.[1] Work undertaken included thousands of miles of minor roads – with accompanying drains, fences and walls – and much land-drainage work. Navigational improvements made to the Shannon included piers, bridges and weirs. Local efforts included the provision of boundary walls around estates and dry-stone walls around fields. Many miles of these had been built early in the eighteenth century and construction continued long after the Famine. The characteristics of local stone and the skills of local workers has left a legacy of regional types of wall, as described in Patrick McAfee's *Irish Stone Walls.*[2]

The nineteenth century saw the establishment of the Commissioners of Public Works (1831), the Institution of Civil Engineers of Ireland (1835), the Royal Institute of the Architects of Ireland (1839) and the first school of civil engineering in Dublin University (Trinity College, 1841). The repeal of the Combinations Acts, the emergence of trade unions, the demise of the craft guilds, the development of employers' associations and the appearance of building-dedicated newspapers, such as *The Irish Builder*, were also of significance.

Agrarian agitation for fairer treatment of tenants, flooding of the market with cheap goods from England and the decline of native industry caused a slowdown in building investment towards the end of the century. The Land Act of 1891 gave tenants assistance in purchasing their holdings, and the century's end saw an improved economy and increased building.

Important research in the early nineteenth century led to the publication of a book on the *Practical Geology and Ancient Architecture of Ireland*,[3] in which the various rock types and their qualities were explored. This book also described the important sources of building stone in each of the 32 counties of Ireland, and provided a record of the sources of stone for particular buildings.

Coastal Defences

The threat of a Napoleonic invasion caused a revival of interest in the fortification of the coast. From 1803 onwards, stone was used for the construction of Martello towers, signal towers and batteries, many of which were abandoned following the

Fig. 78 *Signal tower, Old Head of Kinsale, Co. Cork*

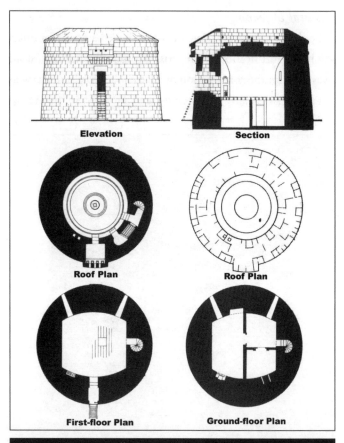

Elevation

Section

Roof Plan

Roof Plan

First-floor Plan

Ground-floor Plan

Fig. 79 *Bullock Martello tower, Co. Dublin*

end of the Napoleonic Wars in 1815. About 50 Martello towers were built, beginning around 1804; they seem to have been built under the general guidance of the military, but the fact that many were under construction at the same time and the differences in detail suggests that local masons had a say in the final design. An example of a signal tower is shown in Figure 78; Figure 79[4] shows the Martello tower at Bullock near Dalkey in County Dublin, and Figure 80 shows the distribution of the signal towers and gives an idea of how significant they were from the perspective of the local stone industry.

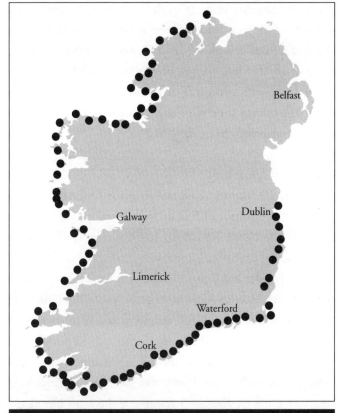

Fig. 80 *Signal towers around the coast, 1804–06*[5]

The rebellion of 1798 had led to a military road being constructed across the Wicklow Mountains, and along this route a string of defensible barracks, built largely of local stone, was completed by 1803. Surrounded by outer walls with bastion-shaped projections at diagonally opposite corners, musket loops in these projections facilitated flank defence.[6]

Fortification of coasts and work on inland waterways kept the stone industry busy up to the middle of the nineteenth century. The pier-head battery at Kingstown (now Dún Laoghaire) was completed in 1857, and though the appearance in 1870 of long-range guns on iron-clad ships demonstrated the ineffectiveness of such fortifications, new batteries were constructed at Belfast Lough, Bere Island, Lough Swilly and Templebreedy in Cork.

Docks and Harbours

Docks and harbours remained of great significance, and further development of Dublin Port saw the completion in 1825 of the North Bull Wall: 1,676 metres of stone wall, comprised of rubble limestone with granite facing. Designed by Francis Giles and George Halpin, the top of the landward portion was built to high-water level, while the outer 152 metres was built to half full-tide level and is submerged at high tide. The resulting increase in velocity in the channel between the North and South Bull Walls caused significant scouring of silt and sand, and was successful in deepening the navigable channel and removing the sand bar at the entrance to the Port of Dublin.

John Rennie, Senr., was responsible in the 1820s for the building of the great tobacco warehouse known as Stack A: 145 metres long, it had four bays of 46.9 metres width. So big was this space that it was used as the location for celebrations to mark the return of the heroes of the Crimean War in 1856. The vaults, which survive, consist of masonry arches supported on masonry walls, with internal columns of granite in a single piece from foundation to springing of the vaults. In 1821, George's Dock – 97.5 metres by 7.6 metres – was completed, and 1824 marked the completion of the Inner Dock – 169.5 metres by 85 metres; both had tidal locks through which ships could pass when the tides were favourable. The masonry was, and continues to be, of the highest quality.

The harbour at Howth, developed as a mail port between 1807–13, used local stone faced with Dalkey granite that was shipped across Dublin bay. Around 1812, Rennie used 4-ton blocks of Runcorn stone to prepare the foundations for the pier heads. This stone was soft and easily cut into blocks, and had the additional quality of hardening when submerged in seawater. On this foundation, header and stretcher courses of stone were laid in mortar (in stretcher courses, the stone is laid with its longest dimension in the direction of the wall face; in header courses, the longest dimension is laid across the wall). Rennie was also responsible for Dún Laoghaire harbour from 1817–21, and upon his death was succeeded by his son. The final form of Dún Laoghaire harbour was not completed until 1860.[7] The stone for its piers was quarried nearby at

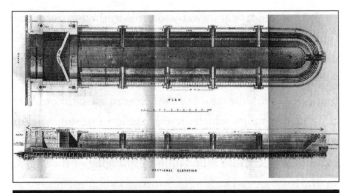

Fig. 81 *Plan and longitudinal section of Graving Dock, Dublin*

Dalkey and transported to the site in 25-ton trucks on a funicular train of six trucks connected to a continuous chain, the weight of the descending loaded trucks hauling the empty ones back up the hill.

The provision of facilities for the maintenance of ships – dry docks – commenced in Dublin Port with Graving Dock no. 1. Built by William Dargan between 1853–60, it is 125

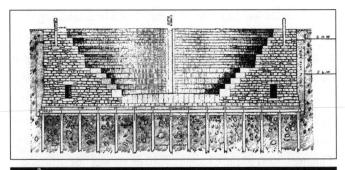

Fig. 82 *Cross section of Graving Dock, Dublin*

metres long and 18.8 metres wide at the entrance, and was considered to be an excellent example of material and workmanship at the time. Figure 81 is an illustration from the

Fig. 83 *The* Mona Brake *in the Graving Dock, Dublin*

archives of the Institution of Engineers of Ireland showing the plan and longitudinal section of the Graving Dock, while Figure 82 shows the cross section of the dock to a larger scale. It was constructed on top of a piled foundation consisting of 300-millimetre-square timber piles averaging 9 metres long at 2.2 metres centres (spacing), with a grillage of timber held down to the piles by 1.5-metre-long screws. Concrete fill was placed between these to the top of the grillage, and a flooring of 100-millimetre planks was spiked down over the whole area. This was designed to act as a unit in resisting upward hydrostatic pressure, and the stonework was built from this prepared base. Figure 83 shows the sailing ship *Mona Brake* undergoing maintenance work in the Graving Dock. Though comfortably accommodated, advances in ship design and size made modifications to the dock necessary almost as soon as it opened. Paddle steamers were commissioned to deliver mail from and to Holyhead, and later – in 1860 – it was necessary to alter the internal shape of the dock walls to accommodate the paddles.

Canals

Hotels and harbours were built on the Grand Canal at Portobello in 1805, and at a number of other locations along the route of the canal. Figure 84 shows people enjoying the Grand Canal Harbour and Hotel at Robertstown in County Kildare in more recent times.

The Royal Canal finally reached the Shannon in 1817, the later sections having been completed under the control of

Fig. 84 *Grand Canal, Robertstown, Co. Kildare*

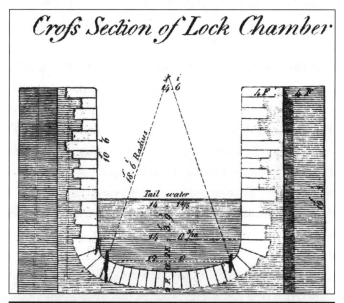

Fig. 85 *Section through lock chamber on the Royal Canal, Dublin*

the Commissioners of Inland Navigation. Figure 85 shows some of the details included in the contract documentation provided by John Killaly, the engineer.

The Ulster Canal was constructed between 1825–42, with locks, bridges, quays, basins and storehouses being constructed of limestone quarried in and around Benburb.[8] The Ballinamore–Ballyconnell Canal – constructed from 1846–59 – included locks of first-class rubble masonry strengthened with cut-stone bonds. The sills, breasts, hollow quoins and coping were of cut stone. The lifts of the locks varied from 1.5–3.4 metres. The locks were 24.7 metres long in the chamber and 5 metres wide, with 1.7 metres of water on the sills.[9]

Railways

The days of the canals drew to a close as the first public railway – the Stockton and Darlington – arrived on the scene in 1825. In Ireland, William Dargan recruited a workforce of 1,000, among them experienced navvies from England, and set about cutting the route from Dublin to Kingstown (Dún Laoghaire). Stone excavated during this operation was used to build bridges, retaining walls and high-quality stations calculated to attract customers from both the wealthy and the working population. Dargan's first train went into service on 17 December 1834.

Political manoeuvring attended the development of the railways, as rival companies jockeyed for public and political support. The Dublin–Belfast route commenced in 1837 at

Fig. 86 *Craigmore Viaduct, Co. Armagh*

the Belfast end, with Dargan to the fore and George Stephenson as supporting consultant. Up to 3,000 men were employed on the project. Completion of the line required the construction of Craigmore Viaduct (Figure 86) the longest and highest viaduct in the country, and which carried the railway over the Camlough River in Armagh. Designed by Sir John McNeill and built of the local grandiorite stone, it is gently curved on plan, has eighteen arches of 18 metres span, and is between 21–43 metres in height. From the Dublin end of the line, an entirely different group was working its way to Drogheda. By 1842, trains were running to Skerries and, by 1844, had reached Drogheda. Unfortunately, the gauge of the two railways was different, and there were many other organisational and administrative problems to overcome before the journey from Dublin to Belfast by rail finally became possible in 1855 with the completion of the Boyne Viaduct, County Louth (Figure 87). Composed largely of local limestone and admired for its

Fig. 87 *Boyne Viaduct, County Louth*

lattice girders (replaced in 1932), it also boasts fifteen semi-circular arches, each of 18.3 metres clear span. The railway boasted many fine stone structures, among them viaducts, bridges, retaining walls, station buildings, signal cabins, sheds and several other miscellaneous accommodation buildings.

Fig. 88 *Kingsbridge/Heuston Station, Dublin*

The terminus at Great Victoria Street in Belfast – since demolished – was a fine building.

Among other main lines were those built by the Great Western and Southern Railway (GS&WR) and the Midland Great Western Railway. The Dublin terminus of the GS&WR at Kingsbridge (now Heuston Station) was designed by Sancton Wood and completed in 1848. Figure 88 shows this elaborate stone edifice, which has been

Fig. 89 *Monard Viaduct, Co. Cork*

described as a Renaissance Palazzo, gay and full-blooded, with fruity swags and little domed towers on the wings. At the other end of the line, Cork was reached in 1849. Figure 89 suggests a busy time for the masons in the Cork area around this period, when the Monard Viaduct was constructed adjacent to the road bridge just outside Cork city. Still in use, it measures 110 metres in length.

The completion by the 1890s of the main lines had involved huge effort on the part of railway companies, and provided stone workers with opportunities to build hundreds of bridges, miles of retaining walls, tunnels, stations and workshops. Construction of the branch lines provided further employment. Railways had their golden era and, like the canals, reached a stage when no further serious expansion was practical.

The significance of the canals and railways cannot be measured entirely in terms of travel and commerce; their social significance was immense. Labour unrest inspired by the success of the French Revolution caused great difficulties to men like Dargan. The ban on ordinary workmen organising to fight oppressive employers was lifted in 1824–25, but strikes remained illegal. The guilds were closed to Catholic journeymen, who had been forming illegal combinations against employers for the purpose of advancing wages and conditions. The stone workers were strongly organised in all towns and cities, and formed travelling lodges on major projects. One outcome of these labour activities was the formation of the Stonecutters' Union of Ireland in Cork in 1848, which was quite successful in looking after the needs of the stonecutters. The stonemasons amalgamated with the bricklayers for the same purpose.

The period of the construction of the railways was also a time of famine in Ireland. The railways provided a means of escape for thousands who otherwise would have starved, though it is extraordinary that this misery coincided with such a period of development and investment.

Mills

A high demand for sailcloth during the Napoleonic Wars led the Linen Board to introduce premiums in 1805

> for all machinery which shall be erected, whether
> entirely new or added to old mills, for spinning
> hemp or flax for sailcloth . . . to be worked by
> steam or water, ten shillings per spindle (on secu-
> rity of regular operation).[10]

Numerous industrialists took up this offer, and mills were built or extended in at least nine locations in Ulster. Figure 90 shows a portion of the fine stone mill at Bessbrook in County Armagh – one of the centres to take advantage of

Fig. 90 *Mill buildings at Bessbrook, Co. Armagh*

the premiums. At the height of the milling boom in the North, there were over 70 mills involved in linen/cotton spinning and weaving. Many of these mills were very large and led to the establishment of milling villages. Both mills and villages were built with a mixture of stone and brickwork.

While milling became very much an industry involving many large establishments, there remained numerous smaller mills serving the domestic economy, and the building and maintenance of these mills was of significance to the stone-building community. Table 2 shows the number of mills in each of the four provinces during the period 1800–60.[11] The table divides mills into those serving the corn, flour, brewing and other grain sectors, and those serving sectors such as flax, bleach and beetling.

Table 2: *Number of mills from 1800–60*

Province	Corn, etc.	Flax, etc.
Ulster	735	1024
Munster	357	102
Leinster	774	229
Connacht	275	75

While the millstones were generally imported, the dressing of grooves as the millstones became worn was a specialised job for millwrights.

The use of wind as a power source was still common in the early part of the nineteenth century, and new windmills were built, among them a six-storey windmill at Armagh, constructed in 1810. Figure 91 shows a small mill built at Tacumshin in County Wexford in 1846. Their construction was mainly random rubble with a little dressed stone.

As industrialisation became widespread, chimneys became a feature of the industrial landscape; while many of these were executed in fine brickwork, stone had its share. Figure 92

Fig. 91 *Tacumshin windmill, Co. Wexford*

shows the chimney of the lead-smelting works at Ballycorus in County Dublin, which was constructed on top of a nearby mountain and connected to the works through a long, stone-arched tunnel stretching along the mountain. The chimney at the copper-smelting installation at the mines near Allihies in west Cork is also shown.

Mills, industrialisation and population shifts during the nineteenth century led to a huge demand for water in the towns and cities, and many dams and reservoirs were built.

Fig. 92 *Chimneys at Ballycorus, Co. Dublin (left) and Allihies, Co. Cork*

Most of the dams were earthen structures, but stone pitching of the inner face was often used, and many feature fine stone intake towers, overflow shafts and ancillary structures. The twin-dammed reservoir at Bohernabreena in County Dublin, commissioned in 1887,[12] features fine granite pitching and structures; a granite-lined canal allowed the more brackish water of the upper catchment to bypass the top dam as compensation water for the many mills sited along the Dodder on its way to the sea.

General Building

In addition to the construction projects mentioned above, houses, schools, colleges, workhouses and jails were being built all over the country. Significant buildings in Dublin included Nelson's Pillar (1808), the General Post Office (1814), the Wellington Testimonial (1817), Kingsbridge Station (1845), Broadstone Station (1850), Trinity Museum (1857), Harcourt Street Station (1860), the National Gallery (1864) and the National Library (1885).

As Belfast grew in importance as a business and industrial centre, the buildings under construction involved both stone and brickwork, among them the York Street Spinning Mill (1842), Queen's University (1849), the Northern Bank (1852), the Assembly's College (1853), the Custom House (1857), the Ulster Hall (1860), Clanwilliam House (1864), the Albert Memorial (1866), the Provincial Bank (1867) and a wide range of churches for the five denominations active in the city.

Church and cathedral building was in full swing all across the country, having started even before Catholic Emancipation. Dublin churches from this period include St George's (1802), Chapel Royal (1807), the Pepper Canister (1824), Black Church (1830), Arran Quay (1835), Mariner's Church, Dún Laoghaire (1837), St Audoen's (1841), Rathmines Church (1850), St Nicholas of Myra (1860), Dominic Street Church (1860) and Findlater's Church (1864). Elsewhere in Ireland, ecclesiastical building saw completion of Newry Cathedral (1825), Tuam Cathedral (1827), Carlow Cathedral (1828), St Michael's, Gorey (1842), Enniscorthy Cathedral (1843), Killarney Cathedral (1855), Limerick Cathedral (1856), St Peter's Cathedral, Belfast (1860), St Colman's Cathedral, Cobh (1868), St Fin Barre's Cathedral, Cork (1865), St McCartan's, Monaghan (1872), Thurles Cathedral (1872), St John's Cathedral, Sligo (1875), Maynooth College Chapel (1893) and St Anne's Cathedral, Belfast (1899). Maurice Craig, in *The Architecture of Ireland from Earliest Times to 1880* (London, 1982), provides an overview of church building during this period:

> There are, in round figures, 14,000 parishes in Ireland, and in the century and a half between the Battle of the Boyne (1690) and the Famine (1847) the great majority of these were provided with churches: one (sometimes more) for the Church of Ireland, three or four, as a rule, by and for the Catholics, and a variable number for such

other denominations as the Presbyterians, Moravians, Quakers and Methodists.[13]

Figure 93 shows St Colman's Cathedral in Cobh, County Cork as a single illustration of the quality of work of the period; some of its stone came by sea from the granite quarries at Dalkey in County Dublin.

Whilst it is clear that there was a continuing boom in stone building in the capital and main cities during the nineteenth century, it is also true that other towns and cities were developing and putting great demands on the stone industry. In Galway, for example, large houses for the professional and merchant classes were being built at the same time as such public buildings as Bridge Mills (1800), the courthouse (1812), the Catholic cathedral (1816), Salmon Weir Bridge (1818), Convent of Mercy (1820), University College, Galway (1843), the Franciscan church (1849), the railway station and Great Southern Hotel (1851), the Augustinian church (1855), St Ignatius' Church (1861), Congregational Church (1863), Bank of Ireland (1863), William Smith O'Brien Bridge (1880), St Joseph's Church (1882), the Methodist church (1885), St Mary's Church (1891) and St Mary's College (1910).

A similar story can be told for towns such as Drogheda, where the following public buildings were being constructed: St Peter's Church (1753), Mayoralty House (1765), Tholsel (1770), Corn Exchange (1796), gate to Ball's Grove (1801), St Mary's Church (Church of Ireland, 1807), the Presbyterian

Fig. 93 *St Colman's Cathedral, Cobh, Co. Cork*

church (1826), industrial workers' houses (1850s), Provincial Bank (1860), Boyne Mill (1865), the Augustinian church (1866), the Christian Brothers school (1867), Bank of Ireland (1876), Dominican Church (1878), St Peter's Church (1880), the courthouse (1889) and St Mary's Church (Roman Catholic, 1884).

The building of substantial dwellings to illustrate the status of the owners continued to be a feature of rural Ireland. Many stone edifices created by landowners and businessmen have stood the test of time, among them Johnstown Castle, near Wexford town (Figure 94), which was brought to its current state between 1810–80; in County Armagh, Gosford Castle was built for the Acheson family in 1820, and also in that year, Killruddery House near Bray in County Wicklow was modified to achieve its current grandeur. Glenstall Castle, County Limerick was built for the Barringtons in 1839, Kylemore Abbey was built as a country home for a Manchester businessman in 1846, Castle Dunboy was built for the owners of the copper mines at Allihies in 1867, Castle Leslie was built at Glaslough in County Monaghan in 1870, and Dromore Castle was built for the Pery family in 1873. These are but a few of the private houses built in the nineteenth century.

Winds of Change
Though stone still comprised a significant share of the building industry at the end of the nineteenth century, the brick-laying 'mason' had a growing involvement in general

building, and concrete had started to push stone out of the civil-works area. Bindon Blood Stoney, for example, used large blocks of precast concrete (up to 350 tons in weight) to form the foundations for the North Wall extension at Dublin Port in 1871–75; he employed a floating crane to put them in place.[14] The railways had also used concrete in bridge abutments and viaduct piers. Stone remained, and probably still remains, the premier architectural choice for the exposed faces of buildings, as it is beautiful and durable and can be formed to give crisp, sculptural details. It suffers, however, from being relatively expensive to extract, work and install, and cannot win the battle when cost is the ultimate decider.

Despite the use of competing materials at the end of the

Fig. 94 *Johnstown Castle, Wexford*

nineteenth century, the stone industry still supplied general building work with such things as lintels, sills, steps, quoins and copings, and a perusal of the records of quarries in the Dublin–Wicklow border area shows stone supplied for houses, schools, hospitals, distilleries, breweries, factories, warehouses and offices. Nevertheless, two specific developments had influenced nineteenth-century attitudes towards the use of stone: the invention, or discovery, of the cavity wall,[15] and the appearance of the modernists. The cavity wall removed the need for thick, load-bearing stone blocks, and allowed the use of thin, outer leaves, ultimately leading to a mere skin of stone cladding. Invented in South Australia around 1860, cavity walls were built in England in the 1890s, and though the traditional solid wall continued here well into the next century, cavity walls eventually became commonplace in Ireland.

As to the modernists – they sought clean lines and planes, with form-following function. To them, stone was fundamentally a compressive material that did not measure up to steel or concrete in terms of its functionality. They also objected to the ornamentation associated so much with classical stone architecture.

8

Mechanisation & Heritage

Stone or Veneer?

The modernists' battle for purity was fought and lost in America and Europe, and a theoretical basis for the 'honest' expression of a stone veneer was reached.[1] Otto Wagner built the Post Office Savings Bank in Vienna with brick in 1906, but with a veneer of marble panels visibly fixed to the brick-work with aluminium-headed iron bolts; Mies van der Rohe used such a system in the Barcelona Pavilion in 1929. Stone was also used as cladding on major multi-storey buildings in New York, among them the Empire State Building of 1931.

The first few years of the twentieth century saw a continu-ation of public and private development. Before 1914, 73 National schools, 37 post offices and twenty coastguard sta-tions had been constructed.[2] However, the First World War of 1914–18, the 1916 Rebellion, the War of Independence (1919–21), the civil war (1922–23), the 'Economic War' (1930s) and the Second World War (1939–45) caused great disruption and changed the stone industry forever. Many skilled men were lost during these momentous events, and by the time the building industry recovered, concrete had largely replaced stone. Stone continued to be in demand at the upper end of the market, and was seen – and is still seen – as having superior aesthetic qualities. It would be wise, however, to acknowledge that great advances have been made in the production of high-quality reconstituted stone, precast concrete and glass-reinforced concrete; these materials have achieved desirable aesthetic qualities that pose a challenge to the use of stone.

Ireland became a member of the European Community in 1973, and a combination of growing prosperity and European support for conservation has led to great investment in the protection of our natural and built environment, with resulting benefits for the building industry in general and the stone sector in particular.

Railways

Though the railways were almost complete by the end of the nineteenth century, small branches were still to be developed, among them the Letterkenny–Burtenport extension (1903), the Rosslare–Waterford extension (1906) and the Armagh–Castleblaney link (1910). Although stone remained a favoured building material for railway structures, brick and concrete were making inroads, not least because brick arches were cheaper than stone; Figure 95 shows the construction of brick arches and stone piers at the Ballyards Viaduct in County Armagh, which goes over the River Callan on the Castleblaney, Keady and Armagh Railway. Figures 96 and 97 shows this approach being applied to the more substantial

Fig. 95 *Ballyards Viaduct, County Armagh, during construction*

viaduct at Tassagh, County Armagh, but here the piers are of concrete, and only the walls are of stone. A later bridge built near Keady Station in County Armagh was constructed

Fig. 96 *Tassagh Viaduct, Co. Armagh, during construction*

Fig. 97 *Tassagh Viaduct, Co. Armagh, on completion*

almost entirely with concrete, with the exception of the arches, which are of engineering brick.

Additional colliery lines were established during the First World War effort, including links to collieries at Walfield near Athy, County Galway (1918), Castlecomer, County Kilkenny (1920) and Arigna, County Antrim (1920).[3] Though stonework had its share, its use was not hugely significant in these construction projects.

Ecclesiastical Building

One area to experience high demand during the first half of the twentieth century was that of ecclesiastical building. Here, stone still commanded the major part of the market. Stone convents, churches and cathedrals were under construction across the entire country, such as St Columba's,

Kilmacrennan, County Donegal (1903), Loughrea Cathedral, County Galway (1903), St Patrick's Cathedral, Armagh (1904), Teampall Éinde, Spiddal, County Galway (1904), St Paul's, Bray, County Wicklow (1912), Church of the Holy Name, Beechwood Avenue, Dublin (1914), Honan Chapel, University College, Cork (1915), Church of Sacred Heart, Cloghoge, County Down (1916), the basilica at Lough Derg, County Donegal (1931), Limerick's Church of the Immaculate Conception extension (1931), Abbey Church, Mount Melleray, County Waterford (1933), Kilbride Church, County Meath (1933), St Peter and Paul's, Athlone (1937), Mullingar Cathedral, County Meath (1939) and Cavan Cathedral (1942). Most of these were Gothic or classical in design, but an effort was made to revive Hiberno-Romanesque; great thickness was a feature of its walls and its absence at openings in the new work often resulted in an appearance of superficial dressing. Figure 98 shows the Romanesque revival in the Church of the Holy Name, Beechwood Avenue, Dublin, which includes well-wrought features, fine ashlar work and snecked rubble in Wicklow and Dublin granites.

A post-Second World War revival in church building saw completion of projects at Carndonagh in County Donegal and in Dublin's Shankill, Foxrock, Merrion Road, Mount Merrion and Harold's Cross (Figure 99). Church building continued with Dolphin's Barn Church extension (1961), Galway Cathedral (1965), St Teresa's, Sion Mills, County Derry (1966), Burt Church, County Donegal (1967), St Brigid's,

Fig. 98 *Beechwood Avenue Church, Dublin*

Newry, County Down (1969), Garvagh First Presbyterian
Church (1971) and Church of the Four Masters, both in
County Donegal (1975); the trend for stone churches continued up until the slump of the 1980s. Self-supporting outer
leaves were a feature of these churches; in the case of St Brigid's
at Rooney's Meadow in Newry, County Down the blocks were
nominally 75-millimetres-thick, knapped limestone from Top
Quarries of Ballinasloe. The knapping machine used hydraulic

Fig. 99 *Holy Rosary Church, Harold's Cross, Dublin*

pressure to chop long blocks into 75-millimetre slices, resulting in a series of concave/convex laminas. The outer leaf was tied to the inner brickwork using bronze wall ties.

Public Buildings

Work on major public buildings during the twentieth century included the Milltown wing of the National Gallery, Dublin (1903), Belfast City Hall (1906), Government Buildings, Merrion Street, Dublin (1911), the new wing to the Vice-regal Lodge (1911) and University College, Dublin's Earlsfort Terrace (1912), but there was little else until the aftermath of rebellion saw the restoration of buildings such as the General Post Office in Dublin.

One project to give continuous employment was the construction of the Mourne Wall. Conceived by the Belfast and District Water Commissioners to define the catchments of the Silent Valley Reservoir, it was built between 1904–22, and stretches like a great serpent for 35 kilometres across the mountain tops and ridges. The wall of roughly hewn granite is about 500 millimetres wide at the top, tapering to about 700 millimetres at the bottom, and stands between approximately 1.2 metres and 2.0 metres high, depending on the undulation of the terrain. The wall top is finished with rough capstones, making its top almost flat enough to walk along, thus affording ramblers shelter from the strong winds of Mourneland. It is a significant monument to the men who quarried the stone from sources adjacent to the wall along the mountainside, and who worked and erected it.

Fig. 100 *Department of Industry and Commerce, Dublin*

The War of Independence (1919–21) led to more restoration work. The upturn also saw construction of City Hall, Cork (1933), Stormont Castle, Belfast (1932), Royal Dublin Society, Dublin (1942) and the Department of Industry and Commerce, Dublin (1942; Figure 100). The Obelisk on Leinster Lawn in Dublin was constructed in 1950.

University College, Dublin's Earlsfort Terrace was one of the last major buildings in which solid-stone external walls were used. Though the advantages of cavity walls had been recognised, solid masonry was still used in housing as late as the 1940s. Nevertheless, the end was in sight for solid work; from here on, stone – where it was used – became firstly the self-supporting outer leaf in a cavity wall and then a panel supported on various fixings. Internal decorative stone slabs were traditionally fixed using dabs of adhesives, but when this technique was applied to external work, failures due to movement quickly brought an end to this practice.

An industrial-development drive led in 1969 to the merging of An Foras Tionscal and the Industrial Development Authority, and the construction of factories and speculative office buildings. Little stone was used, and only as external cladding rather than as an integral part of the structure. When Irish architecture needed stone cladding, the industry produced the machinery to manufacture it and the fixings to secure it. Firms such as Stone Developments Ltd. (established in 1965) supported the building professions with the provision of working details from their drawing offices.

The modernist ethic was expressed in thin cladding in many buildings from the 1960s onwards. In Dublin, the technique was applied at the Science Building in UCD (University College, Dublin), Bord na Mona's headquarters, Bank of Ireland at Baggot Street, ESB (Electricity Supply Board) head office at Fitzwilliam Street, College of Technology in Kevin Street, Carroll's Building on the Grand Canal, Donnybrook Fire Station and the College of Technology, Bolton Street. The Universal Insurance head-quarters in Shannon also reflected the new approach. Traditionally competing materials – concrete and stone – came together in both the Central Bank Building in Dublin's Dame Street and in Dublin's Civic Offices, where precast panels were given a granite face; thin granite slabs were placed in the casting moulds with grouted stainless-steel rods protruding, after which the concrete panels were poured, giving an integral granite finish.

Conservation and New Work

The recession in the 1980s hit the stone industry hard, and the commencement of restoration work on the Bank of Ireland in College Green and Dublin's Custom House was welcomed. Figure 101, showing the coat of arms of Ireland at roof level on the river front over the Custom House, illustrates the quality of handwork achieved in the restoration project. These projects contributed substantially to the regeneration of the old handcraft, and the industry went forward

Fig. 101 *Custom House, Dublin (detail)*

in a more confident mode, knowing that it could serve modern demands whilst maintaining the stock of existing stone buildings. Recent years have seen considerable investment in conservation and restoration of a wide range of old stone buildings, among them Trim Castle, County Meath (1993), Collins Barracks, Dublin (1994) and Ardfert Cathedral, County Galway (1999). The Office of Public Works and Dúchas, the state heritage service, initiated much of this work, but private investment in the conservation of listed buildings was also significant. This work acknowledges stone's aesthetic and historical value and now constitutes an important outlet for the stone industry.

Some parts of the stone industry have invested in high-output machinery and have taken advantage of the wider European market, with Belgium now a major destination. Belgian limestone sources are no longer workable, and Irish limestone – having similar characteristics – has satisfied some of that country's demand; indeed, one Irish producer has established itself in Belgium through company acquisitions. Confidence in stone extraction and working has also led to Irish 'experts' being able to offer their services to Ireland's overseas-aid programme, and they have assisted the emerging stone industries in Third World countries.

Traditional solid work still arises in important restoration projects, and where clients or architects consider it appropriate or desirable, but the high cost of producing cut stone from Irish sources has led to substitution from cheaper sources, and much of our stonework is now based on imported material.

Fig. 102 *Millennium Wing, National Gallery, Dublin*

The architects and client for the prestigious Millennium Wing at the National Gallery in Dublin (Figure 102) have chosen an imported Portland stone, rain-screen cladding as an integral part of the design of the façade. This building, placed in the context of a Georgian street scape, needed some monumentality in order to achieve an impact in that street scape. The nature of the spaces and their usage precluded the proliferation of windows of Georgian façades, but stone, counterpoised against the brickwork of the street achieved the required impact. Gordon Benson appraised the project in *Irish Architect* (Dublin, March 2002):

> Apertures within the wall offer highly specific
> views of Trinity College and Clare Street/Nassau

Street. These moments anchor in the visual
memory of the visitor meaningful relationships
between the building, the artefacts it houses and
the specific urban context within which they exist.[4]

The fact that stone was chosen for a building of such national
importance is a good omen for its place in future projects.

An example of stone cladding used to enhance a commercial development in Ballsbridge, Dublin is shown in
Figure 103. For this showroom/office/shop complex,
imported polished granite was used: Spanish Rosa Porino
and Scandinavian Balmoral cladding, both pink in colour.

The close of the twentieth century saw the stone industry
become increasingly mechanised as it sought to maintain and
expand its market. The demand for high-class cladding and
flooring persists in up-market building sectors, such as public

Fig. 103 *Modern commercial development, Dublin*

buildings, commercial developments, corporate headquarters and in hotel and leisure-complex sectors. Stone has established its reputation for quality and durability, and remains one of the noble materials. Those involved in designing, working and building in stone look forward with well-founded confidence.

Appendix

An Gobán Saor

The most famous of the Irish builders was the Gobán Saor, the great master mason of Irish antiquity. He is stated to have built many great buildings; indeed, one could almost say that any stone structure of note will have been attributed to him at one time or another. If it collapsed it was not his work, and if it lasted then there was no possibility that anyone else could have built it. He is mentioned in connection with building for the saints in eighth-century texts, and scholarly discourses of the nineteenth century attributed works to him, located his birthplace, identified his parentage and told of his burial place. Current wisdom sees him as an important myth derived from Goibhniu, the smith god. A ninth-century poem refers to the constructor of the firmament as Gobán, and makes it clear that he was considered the original master builder.[1] The stories of the early Irish saints are full of marvels, but usually there is some truth embedded within them; nevertheless, I am reluctant to allow rationalism to eliminate the Gobán. Imponderables such as 'truth' can get in the way of the enjoyment of good stories, and there are many related to the Gobán Saor. *Duine glic do bhí sé*, he outsmarted kings, monks and others who would have cheated him. It is peculiarly Irish that the Gobán should have been equated with God, since elsewhere in Europe there was a great reluctance even to use the term 'architect' because it was held that there was only one and He was the architect of the universe.

The traditional stories of the Gobán Saor are modified in various regions, but there are more or less constant issues.

Gobán's Birthplace

Petrie gives reasons why he considered the Gobán Saor to be a historically real person who was born at Turvey in north County Dublin.[2] He bases his assertion on extant versions of the Books of Lecan and Ballymote, in which the Gobán's father is identified. Speaking of Turvey Strand, these books say, 'Traig Turbi, whence was it named? Not difficult. Turbi Traghmar, the father of Gobán Saor, was he who had possession of that land.' Petrie dates the period of the Gobán Saor's activities to the seventh century from references to churches and towers of that period: the wooden *duirteach* of St Molling (now St Mullin's in County Carlow; Figure 104) and towers at Kilmacduach, Killala, Antrim and possibly Glendalough have been attributed to the Gobán Saor in both literature and traditions of these areas.

Birth of the Gobán's Son

The Gobán Saor and his wife were living together in a particular town and another married couple were living near them in the same town. The Gobán's wife had three or four daughters, and the other man's wife had three or four sons. It happened that both women were expecting at about the same time, and they planned that if the Gobán's wife had a daughter and the other woman had a son that they would exchange them unknown to the husbands or anybody else. When the children were born, the Gobán's wife had a daughter and the other woman had a son. They made the exchange unknown to anybody, and there was rejoicing in every house because the Gobán had a son and because there was a daughter in the other house. They grew up until the Gobán's son was a young man, but the Gobán had his doubts and, as the story develops, he arranges for the son to marry a very smart girl who turns out to be his daughter.

Fig. 104 *St Mullin's, Co. Carlow*

Marriage of the Gobán's Son

The story of the Gobán's marriage takes different twists in different parts of the country, but the central theme is constant.

When the Gobán was getting old, he was worried about his son and wanted him to marry well so he would have the support of a strong wife. He told his son to go to the fair one day and gave him a sheepskin. 'Take that,' says he, 'and bring me home the skin and the price of it.' Wool was very dear at that time.

The son did as he was told, brought with him the skin and walked up and down the fair. He was the laughing stock of the fair when he asked his price. At last, as evening was drawing nigh, a young girl of nice appearance came over to him and took the skin. She got a scissors, plucked the wool off it and kept it, and then she gave him back the skin and the price of it. The Gobán's son was satisfied and he went home. He told the father all that had happened, and the father asked him would he know the girl again if he met her, and he said he thought he would.

'Well now,' says the father, 'I would want to see you married before I die and as you are passing your teens and looking out for a wife I wouldn't be satisfied with any other girl except that one. I would like her to come and visit my house, but on condition that she will not come by day or night, not come by road or by field, and not come alone nor yet have anyone with her.'

The Gobán's son brought her the message next day and he was greatly puzzled. He thought she would never understand his father's message. As for himself, he was blind to it alto-gether. 'Don't worry,' said the girl. 'I will manage that without any trouble.'

So this is what she did. She came in the twilight, and she came along the fences, and she brought a dog with her so that she wasn't alone. When the Gobán's father saw the way she carried out his message, he was very proud of her and told his son that she was the girl for him to marry, and that he wouldn't be satisfied with anyone else.

So, to shorten the story, the day of their marriage was arranged and they were married. The old Gobán was satisfied when he saw his son settle down with a clever wife.

The Wisdom of the Wife of the Gobán's Son

The Gobán and his son had a job to attend to for Mallick, who lived some distance away. On the first day that the Gobán and his son set out on the road, they had not gone very far when the father said, ' Shorten the road my son.'

'Begad, I cannot shorten it,' the son said.

'Oh, if that is the way we might as well go home,' the father said, 'because we will not do any good today.'

They came home, and when they came in again the young woman asked the young man what brought them home. 'My father asked me to shorten the road,' he said, 'and when I said I could not do that he said we might as well return home.'

'Ah, you fool,' she said. 'If he asks you to shorten it again, start to tell him a story.' And she told him a story he could tell to his father. The next day the son did as she said, and the father went all the way and the job was done.

The Gobán was getting old at this time and deteriorating. His son's wife knew he would not live much longer. One day, she asked her husband if he knew his craft well now, and he said there was nothing he did not know about starting or finishing a job. 'You fool,' she said. 'You will never do any good. Go out tomorrow morning and come back after a while shouting and clapping your hands. Your father will ask you what is wrong with you, and then you say there is not a stone upon a stone from top to bottom of Mallick's court.'

The son did this. He came in to his father the following day, making an uproar. 'What's wrong with you?' When he told the father about Mallick's court, he did not believe him and replied: 'A house that had *caid ar caid* [a stone upon stone], *gá caid ar caid* [two stones upon a stone] *agus caid idir gá caid* [and a stone between two stones], how could it fall?'

This triad described the Gobán's method and the son got an insight into how to build houses. He was successful from then on. Be that as it may, the secret of the Gobán's method still eludes other masons, and many a pint has been downed while trying to grasp it.

The Gobán Pleases Himself

The Gobán was a mason and there was no better man at his craft. He once made a stone chest and left it on the side of the road in public view and hid nearby so he would hear people's opinion of it as they went by. The majority thought it was fine, except that the legs were too long under it. The Gobán took it and he shortened the legs somewhat. He put it back in the same place and went into hiding near it again. It was not long until a group of people went by, and they took an interest in it, and they were of the opinion that it was a fine piece except that the legs were too short. The Gobán then knew he would be a fool to try and please everyone.

The Gobán and the Little People

One autumn evening, the Gobán Saor was sitting on the grass alone under a big chestnut tree. The sun was sloping down behind the hill, and as he sat there thinking for himself, he was disturbed by a little man not much bigger than his knee who spoke to him.

'Is there anything troubling you now Gobán,' said the little man.

'Not much,' said the Gobán, 'but only one thing – I wish I was able to buy a new pair of tools for working.'

'Well,' said the little man, 'don't get downhearted. I will help you. The next time you come here, bring your tools with you and I will be waiting for you.'

'If I went home now and brought them here would it do?'

'Well,' says the little man, 'you better wait until the sun will be sloping down tomorrow evening because that is the only time we are allowed to show ourselves to men.'

'And is there any harm to ask you,' said the Gobán, 'what do you want of them?'

'Well,' says the little man, 'I will sharpen them for you,

and put some magic on them, and they will be better a thousand times than any tool you could buy in the shop.'

The next evening, the Gobán brought the tools to the big chestnut tree, and he hadn't long to wait when he heard the little man coming down the tree and a little wee bag on his back. The while he was sharpening them with an instrument, he told the Gobán a very strange story. He told him that his wife would have a young baby boy and that he too, when he would grow up, would have the same power to use these tools and instrument, and that he would have only to touch the part he wanted to sharpen with the instrument and it would work like magic. 'But,' says he, 'there is one condition you mist fulfil. You must not tell anyone that you saw me or that I sharpened them for you. Don't tell your wife either, and don't give any one of them away to another neighbour, because if you do the magic will go and they will be as any other instruments. Rust will eat them and they will fall to pieces.'

So the Gobán promised him he would do everything he said and wouldn't tell anybody about them. He thanked him and bade good evening to him and went home. He saw the little man climbing up the big chestnut tree and disappearing from sight.

When the Gobán came home, his wife saw him having his kit on his back and she asked him where he was, and he said he was back at such-and-such a man doing a little job for him, so she didn't put the story further and left it so.

About a month from that day, didn't the little man's word come true. His wife had a baby boy and he was overjoyed. So overjoyed was he that he was about to tell her about the secret the little man told him, but something caught his breath and he didn't tell her.

Everything passed on well, day after day, week after week, month after month, until the baby boy grew up to manhood and was able to take his father's place. The old man himself

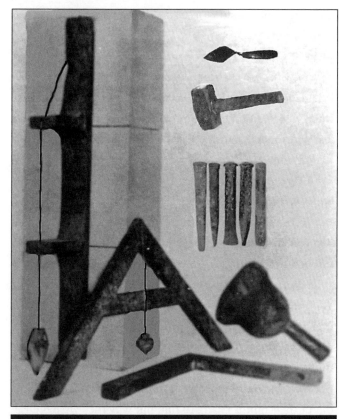

Fig. 105 *Old masons' tools*

was not able to work hard, but he used to accompany his son from place to place. Anywhere a building was to be done, the father used to be with him, but he kept his secret secret and brought it to the grave with him. He knew as long as the son wouldn't give away the tools to anybody – as he warned him from time to time not to give, but never told him why – that the son would understand that there was something the matter and would be as true to his word as he himself was to his secret.

The Gobán and the Round Towers[3]

It so happened that the Gobán Saor was out walking one day when who should he see approaching but an old man with a bag on his back, and he bent down to the ground with the weight of it.

'A very good day to you,' says the old man. 'Are you going far?'

'To the high field to turn home the cow,' says the Gobán. 'Do you know me?' For the old man was driving the two eyes through him.

'I don't,' says the old man, 'but I knew your father well.' With that, he left down the bag and sat on top of it. 'It was ever said that your father would have a son whose name would be the Gobán Saor, and this son would build the round towers in Ireland – monuments that would stand the test of time, and the people in future generations would go out of their minds trying to find out why they were built in the first place. One day, the Gobán Saor would meet an old

Fig. 106 *Base of the round tower at St Mullin's, Co. Carlow*

man who would be carrying on his back the makings of his famous monuments. Did your father ever tell you that?'

'He did not,' says the Gobán, 'for he is dead with long.'

'I think I'll be soon joining him,' says the old man, 'but I have one job to do before I go. Where would you like to build your first round tower?'

'I'm going to the high field to turn home the cow,' says the Gobán, 'so I might as well build it there.'

They went to the high field and the stranger drew a circle with his heel around where the cow was grazing. He opened his bag and they dug out the foundations. Then he gave the Gobán Saor his traps: trowel, hammer, plumb-rule and bob, and he showed him how to place a stone upon a stone: where to look for the face of the stone and where to look for the bed, where to break the joint and where to put in a through bond.

The wall wasn't long rising, and as the wall rose, the ground inside the wall rose with them, and they were a good bit up before they thought of the door, and they put in a window when they felt like it. When they got thirsty, they milked the cow and killed the thirst. The tower tapered as they went up, and when they thought they were high enough the Gobán came out of the top window to put the coping on the tower. By this time, the field was black with people all marvelling at the wonder. The Gobán's mother was there and she called out, 'Who's the young lad on top of the steeple?'

'That's your own son,' they told her.

'Come down,' says she, 'and turn home the cow!'

On hearing his mother, the Gobán Saor climbed in the window. The ground inside the tower lowered down with him. When he was passing the door high up in the wall, the Gobán jumped and the cow jumped and the old man jumped, and that was the jump that killed him and he is buried where he fell, the first man in Ireland with a round tower as his headstone; Daniel O'Connell was the second.

The Gobán picked up his bag of tricks, and after he turned home the cow, his mother washed his shirt and baked a cake, and he went off raising round towers up and down the country.

The Gobán in Danger

When the Gobán Saor had finished the round towers in Ireland, he turned his hand to building palaces, castles and big houses, and every one he built was finer than the one before.

You'd think that a young woman would be worried that her husband might be led astray by girls he might meet on travels away from home, but not the Gobán's son's wife. She told him, 'Anywhere you go, be friendly with any girl you meet, and any story you hear keep it in your head. You'd never know when your father might want you to shorten the road.'

One day, they took the road to a gentleman's place in the west of Ireland because a new big house was wanted. The son shortened the road with an occasional story. The house was to be five-storeys high, bigger and better than anything in the district. They started the work, and they were building and building until they almost had it completed. The Gobán's son became fairly friendly with the daughter of the house during that period, and one day she told him that the master of the house intended to kill the Gobán when the house was finished for fear that he would build another and finer house in the same district. The son told the story to his father, and he was as vigilant as he could be. He was in no hurry to finish the house, and the gentleman used to come to him very frequently asking him when it would be ready. One morning that he came to question him, the Gobán said that he would have to go home to collect three tools before he could finish the house and that there was no way in which he could finish the house without them. The gentleman was suspicious that if the Gobán got home he would not return at all, and he said to the Gobán to send his own son for them. 'I will not indeed,' said the Gobán, 'because he is not very intelligent and I would be afraid that he would break them and they are very expensive. And furthermore, no one else knows where they are or what they are called except myself and my son's wife.'

The gentleman did not want to let the Gobán home, and he said to him to write down the names of the three tools on a piece of paper and that he would send his own son for them to the Gobán's house. The Gobán did this, and the gentleman's son went with the piece of paper, and what was written on it, *as gaeilge,* was, 'One turn for another. Tit for tat. Wait until you get.' These were the names of the three tools, and the Gobán knew that his son's wife would know that he was in danger.

When the gentleman's son reached the Gobán's house, he handed the piece of paper to the woman of the house and asked her to give him three tools that were named on the piece of paper because the Gobán wanted them to finish his father's house.

The woman looked at the piece of paper and understood what was afoot. Off with her to the big chest which was in the corner of the house in which the Gobán's tools used to be kept. The chest was almost as high as herself and, after searching for a considerable time, she said to the gentleman's son that she could not reach the tools, that they were at the bottom of the chest and that he would have to go into it himself to get them. In he went and he stooped down to get them. When she got him bent down, she closed the lid tightly on him and she put the lock on the chest and left him there.

When the gentleman tired of waiting for his son's return, he asked the Gobán what was keeping him. The Gobán said that he would not get sight of him until he (the Gobán) was let home. The gentleman had to let the Gobán and his son go home, and to pay them their money to the last farthing.

Gobán's Wages

The Gobán Saor was a great builder but his charges were not small and he sometimes fell out with his clients. He once built a monastery, but when it was almost completed the monks tried to lower his wages. He refused to renegotiate the arrangement, but they waited until he was on top of the building and they removed all the ladders and scaffolding. They said they would not allow him to descend unless he agreed to their proposal. The clever Gobán, however, began to throw down stone after stone of the building, saying that this was as easy a way as any to descend safely to the ground. Whereupon the monks relented and agreed to pay his full wages.

Blessing the Gobán

Gobán was a member of St Madhóg's community, and after the saint blessed his hand, he built a church with wonderful carvings in it. So deft and accurate was he that he could drive nails into the top of a high building without any climbing. He would throw the nail in the air, throw the hammer after it so that it would strike the nail into the proper place, and then catch the hammer again before it reached the ground.

The Gobán and St Abban

In the early life of St Abban, it is said that there was a distinguished builder residing convenient to St Abban and Gobán was his name; and it was his constant occupation to do the work of the saints in every place where they were until, at length, he had lost his sight because of the displeasure of the saints on account of his dearness and the greatness of his charges. St Abban went to him to ask him to build a church for him. Gobán told him that it was not possible because of his being blind. St Abban said to him, 'You shall get your sight while you are doing the work, and it shall go from you again when you have finished the work.' And so it was done, and the name of God, and of St Abban, were magnified by this.

The Gobán at St Mullin's

The story of the building of the wooden oratory, Teach Moling, for St Molling at St Mullin's in County Carlow is told in an early life of the saint.

St Molling brought the Gobán Saor to build his oratory and said that he would pay whatever the Gobán asked for the work. The Gobán's company consisted of eight carpenters and their wives and eight boys. The Gobán's wife received a present of a cow from the saint, but it was stolen and she complained to the saint. The saint's searchers found the thief roasting his cow at a large fire by the Barrow. He climbed a tree but he was wounded and fell into the river and drowned. The party took the half-burned cow back, and the saint prayed over it and it was restored.

The Gobán's wife asked for the return of the cow but the saint did not comply and she returned to her husband in anger. She made the Gobán agree to let her determine the price he should ask for the building work, and he agreed. She asked for the full of the oratory with rye, and this was what Gobán demanded of the saint. The saint said he would comply if the Gobán inverted the oratory so that it could be filled. Gobán applied machinery and force to the oratory so that he turned it upside down without disturbing a plank.

The demand was a great blow to the saint but he contacted all his friends and relations and managed to fill the oratory with every kind of grain and the Lord turned these into rye for the Gobán Saor. Having taken his rye away, the Gobán Saor found it reduced the following day to nothing but maggots.

Poem of Suibne Geilt

A poem, contained in an eighth-century Irish manuscript from a monastery in Carinthia and attributed to Suibne Geilt, who ended his life in Teach Moling, shows astrology in vogue in the early Irish Church. Some of the words are archaic but the Gobán is mentioned.[4]

> Suibne, the mad, Barr Edin
> A Mairiu I have heard in Tuaim Inbir
> Nor is there a house more auspicious
> With its stars last night
> With its sun, with its moon.

Gobban made there
A black Conecestar and a tower
My believing in the God of Heaven
That raised the choicest towers.
The house of the Ire Fera Flechod
The house of the chief Virgin he built
More conspicuous than the orchid's food
And it without an Udnucht upon it.

The Gobán at Holycross

The Gobán was a proud man and he could easily get into a huff. When the old abbey of Holycross was building, one bright summer's morning, a middle-aged man, poorly clad, came by. His tools were in his wallet over his shoulder, and he seemed tired and footsore from the heat of the day. 'God bless the work,' says he.

'God bless the spokesman,' says the men who were working away like mad.

'I'm on tramp,' says he to the master mason, 'and maybe you could give me a job to help me on my way.'

'What are you able to do?' says the master.

'Wisha, not much,' says the traveller.

'Well,' says the boss – who was a conceited sort of a fellow – 'you look like it. But I'll give you a trial. We're just going out for our dinner and there's a fresh stone there on the banker, and cut me out,' says he, 'a cat with two tails.' So saying, he took his mallet and gave warning for dinner.

As soon as their backs were turned, what become the poor

tramp but he threw his wallet on the ground and, taking out his mallet and chisels, he fell to work. Before the dinner hour was over, he had a fine mouser with two tails cut out of the block of stone, so natural that you'd think he was going to fly at you. He then bundled up his tools, threw his wallet over his shoulder and faced for Cashel as fast as he could foot it. He had hardly turned his back when up came the master and his men. 'What's this? By the piper,' says he, 'but sure enough here's a cat with two tails, and beautifully cut it is too.'

The men all gathered round the banker and declared 'twas the finest piece of work they ever laid eyes on. 'Who is he?' says one of them.

'Who is he?' says another.

An old, grey-haired mason, who was in the background, came forward and, when he looked at the piece of work, he slapped his thigh. ''Twas the Gobán Saor himself,' says he. 'There isn't a mortal man living could do it but himself.'

'Boys,' said the master, 'I'm ashamed of myself! Divide yourselves into bands and take to the four cross roads, and bring him back whether he will or no. Sure, he can't be far on his way.'

The men started off and searched the country all round, but sorra a tail or tidings of the Gobán did they get from that day to this. So they had nothing to do but put up the cat with the two tails in the building in remembrance of the Gobán. If you go to Holycross, you'll see it up in the wall of the church to this day.

The Gobán's Residence

The Gobán Saor was a wonderful man. He could build a *caher*, a bridge, a round tower or a castle in the grandest style. He could forge a shield or a helmet, and make the finest tempered swords and spears of any man living. Nothing was beyond him.

He lived at Rath-Gobbin, in the ould castle there – that is, it was once a castle but is nothing now but a few relics of walls. You will see it not far from the road on the left as you go up from Watergrass Hill. 'Tis a lone and dreary place enough now, but believe me, it was warm and comfortable enough when the Gobán kept it with lashings of eating and drinking, and no poor soul ever turned from his gate cold or hungry; and sure, why wouldn't he when he had all the work of the country, far and near, and no one thought a job was well done unless the Gobán had a hand in it. He had one son: a fine strapping comely fellow he was; at dancing or wrestling or hurling he would beat the whole side of the country, and no man could handle a sledge with him.

Now it happened that the ould woman took sick and died, and the Gobán was greatly put about for the loss of his faithful *banatí*; for who was to look after the milkmaids and the dairy women, to see that the cows were properly milked and the keelers scoured, and the milk set, and the butter churned, all in due time and season? And wasn't there the meals to be got ready for the journeymen and the apprentice boys and the farm labourers and servant girls? Believe me, the housekeeping was no joke at Rath-Gobbin. 'So, my boy,' says he to his son one evening when they were having their smoke after supper, 'we are badly off in regard to the house-keeping, everyone pulling and hauling and all sorts of waste and idleness going on, and as I'll never put any woman in your mother's place, I'd wish you to look out for some clean-handed decently reared girl, as it is now high time for you to be married.'[5]

The story of how the marriage was organised has already been told.

The Gobán at Kilgobbin

The Gobán Saor's fame as a wonderful architect was so great that from all parts of the known world came offers and invitations to him to come to the assistance of kings and princes who wished to transmit their names and fame to posterity as founders of remarkable buildings. Many of those calls he obeyed, and fulfilled his tasks to the entire satisfaction of his employers, as was proved by the fabulous wealth with which he was rewarded. Upon one occasion, he was summoned to France to construct some castle for the king of that country and, like a sensible man, knowing the uncertainties of travel and sojourn in foreign parts, before leaving he made his will and had buried his accumulated wealth in one of the vaults of Kilgobbin Castle in County Dublin (Figure 107), then inhabited by some of his family.

Time passed on and he did not return. Many years elapsed before the cause of his continuous absence transpired. The French monarch, more than delighted with the results of

Fig. 107 *Kilgobbin Castle, Co. Dublin*

the Irishman's labour on his behalf, determined that no neighbouring potentate should eclipse him architecturally, at any rate not with the aid of the Gobán Saor. So when that worthy came to bid his royal employer farewell, he was hurried out of the palace and decapitated, and according to one old narrative, 'as men without heads are but indifferent travellers', he never returned to disinter his treasure or make known its whereabouts.

How the idea of its being hidden in Kilgobbin Castle arose it is impossible to say, but implicit faith was placed in the notion that under or near the castle, the gold would one day be found, and locals have often endangered the walls in efforts to find it.

The Gobán's Grave

On an island in a bog in the parish of Greystown, County Tipperary, you can see the slight remains of an important early Irish monastery. This is currently known as Derrynavlan, which is the English form of Daire na Fland or 'Oak-wood of the Ivy'. In the graveyard of the monastery, there are some monuments said to indicate the burial place of the Gobán Saor. One of the stories about the circumstances of his death follows (in the narrative, the name Deirena B'plannc is used, and it was explained as 'the end of the plank', which the narrator thought to relate to the end of a planked road across the bog).

The Gobán Saor and his twelve journeymen, it is said, were waylaid and killed by twelve robbers, who buried or hid their remains in the bog. The culprits made their way to their victim's house; they were received by the widow as if nothing

Fig. 108 *An Gobán Saor's grave slab, Greystown, Co. Tipperary*

had happened, though she had been made aware of the murders. Requesting their assistance to open a piece of oak which her husband had been sawing into a plank, she slyly withdrew the wedge and the heavy planks, springing together, caught their hands as in a vice, when the widow – who was a woman of strength and resolution – cut off their heads with an axe.

She then caused the remains of her husband and his twelve workmen to be interred in Deire-na B'plannc.

There are six slabs in the graveyard and the locals insist that the grave slab shown in Figure 108 is the grave of the Gobán and his wife, and the five others of his men, the rest of the monuments having disappeared.[6]

Glossary

abutment	end support for a bridge
aisle	side passage in a church
ambulatory	covered walkway
annals	records of ancient events in Ireland
antae	projection of side walls through gables in early churches
arcading	succession of arches supported on columns
architraves	moulding frame surrounding a window or door
ashlar walls	walls formed of squared stone
basalt	a volcanic rock
bastion	projecting strong point in a fortification
batter	slight deviation from the vertical causing wall to decrease in thickness with height
battlemented	having a parapet indented or castellated at regular intervals
bearing medium	the ground surface on which a foundation is build
beehive hut	stone hut resembling a conical beehive
beetling	crushing flax in linen manufacture
blind arcade decoration	wall surface decorated with false arches and columns
Boyne culture	neolithic culture of the Boyne valley
cairn	large pile of stones or earth
caisson	watertight open-toped box in which foundations can be built in water
cantilevered	not supported at the outer edge
capital	top section of a stone column
capstone	heavy stone over a portal tomb

cashel	circular stone fort
castellated	having battlements
cathair	circular stone fort or habitation site
caulk	to make watertight using compacted material
Celtic cross	stone cross with circle connecting the arms
chamber	a space having a floor, walls and roof
chancel	the part of church reserved for the altar
circular fort	see cashel
cloigtheach	Irish for round tower, meaning 'bell house'
cloister	enclosed garden and walkway in a monastery
clochán	Irish for beehive hut
Coade stone	a manufactured stone
column capital	see capital
coping	top course in a wall or pier
corbel	stone projection from general surface of a wall
cornice	projecting course of masonry at the top of a building
court tomb	tomb featuring a court outside the entrance
credence niche	niche for sacred vessels
cross-in-circle decoration	decoration composed of a cross inscribed in a circle
decorating	surface enhancing for decorative purposes
dolerite	stone containing felspar and pyroxene
dolmen	name sometimes used for a portal tomb
dry-stone walling	walling using stone without the aid of mortar
dún	Irish for an important dwelling or fort site
earthworks	structure using large earthen embankments
embrasure	opening in a wall to facilitate the firing of guns in defence
funerary structure	structure built primarily as a tomb
gallery	one of several chambers in a gallery tomb
garth	an enclosed garden or space
geometrical patterning	patterns based on geometrical shapes
Gothic	style of architecture featuring high, pointed arches
grillage	grill-like structure
gryke	weathered crack in a limestone surface
header course	masonry course in which the smaller ends of blocks are exposed
Hiberno-Romanesque	Irish development of early European architectural style
high cross	free-standing cross
horse	vertical support for scaffolding

jamb stone	stone forming the jamb of a door or window
jumper	long chisel for drilling stone
keep (castle)	tower or stronghold of a castle
kerb	stone used to define a periphery
La Tène Celts	Celts coming to Ireland from Europe in last centuries BC
Lamina	thin layer
lintel	member carrying masonry over a window or door
low relief	designs lightly carved on a surface
mace-head	head for a ceremonial mace
megalithic	composed of large stones
mica-schist rubble	walling composed of irregular mica-schist stones
mortar carbonate	salts derived from the setting of mortar
murage	tax to finance the construction of protective walls
nave	the wide central part of a church
neolithic	pertaining to the late Stone Age
Newgrange	a passage grave in the Boyne Valley
ogham	early form of writing using strokes on the edges of stones
oolite limestone	granular form of limestone
ordered chancel arch	arch having several steps in its cross section or profile
orthostat	vertical stone
outcrop	projecting from the general terrain
over-sailing	projecting with outer edge unsupported
passage grave	tomb approached through a passage
passage-grave art	art found in megalithic tombs
paving	stone surface of road, yard or footpath
pick-dressed	surface textured using a stone pick
pillar stone	standing stone
piscine niche	niche for washing sacred vessels
plumb line	device for defining a vertical line using a hanging weight
pontage	tax to finance the construction of bridges
portal tomb	tomb entered through a large portal, often called a dolmen
post-hole	hole left in the ground where vertical supports once stood
profile	cross section showing shapes of intersecting surfaces

projection	parts jutting out from a surface
promontory fort	fort built on a promontory so that only the landward side needs protection
quadripartite vault	vault having four sides
quoin	stone forming corner in a wall
rampart	protective embankments
random rubble	walling composed of irregular stones of various sizes
Renaissance	period of rebirth of art, science and culture in Europe
revetment	earth-retaining wall
ringfort	circular fort or protected habitation site
rock art	early designs cut in the surfaces of exposed native rock
Romanesque	early architectural style developed in Europe
round tower	bell tower or refuge in a monastery
sally point	point from which to launch a counter attack
sculpture in the round	three-dimensional sculpture
scutching mill	a mechanical means for separating flax fibres from the skin and pith of the plant
sedelia	recessed seats in the sanctuary of a church
sett	small paving stone
silicosis	lung disease caused by breathing in silica
sill stone	stone threshold at entrance
slype	covered passage, usually leading to cloister
snecked rubble	form of rubble walling in which the stones are split and the split faces exposed
souterrain	man-made subterranean passage, chamber or cave
squared rubble	walling composed of squared stones of various sizes
statuary	statues
stretcher course	masonry course in which the long faces of blocks are exposed
trapezoidal chamber	chamber having irregular straight surfaces
vaulted	covered with an arched roof
viaduct	bridge carrying a road or railway across a valley
wedge-shaped tomb	tomb having wedge-shaped chambers
winter solstice	period around 21–22 December each year
wrought stone	stone hewn into a chosen shape

Notes & References

Chapter 1: Prehistoric Stone Buildings
1 O'Kelly, M.J., *Early Ireland,* Cambridge, 1989, p. 85.
2 Ibid. p. 92.
3 Ibid. p. 97.
4 Ibid. p. 115.
5 Herity, M. and Eoghan, G., *Ireland in Prehistory*, Routledge and Kegan Paul, London, 1977, p. 65.
6 O'Connell, J.W. and Korff, A., *The Book of the Burren,* Tír Eolas, Kinvara, County Galway, 2001, p. 62.
7 O'Kelly, M.J., *Newgrange, Archaeology, Art and Legend,* Thames and Hudson, 1982, pp. 116–21.
8 O'Sullivan, Dr M., *Megalithic Art in Ireland,* Town House and Country House, Dublin, 1993, p. 10.
9 Kelly, F., *A Guide to Early Irish Law,* Dublin, 1988, p. 30.
10 MacNeill, E., *Ancient Irish Law,* PRIA, 36c, 1923, p. 305.

Chapter 2: Stone Decoration & Sculpture
1 Finlay, I., *Celtic Art,* Faber and Faber, London, 1973, p. 170.
2 Herity, M. and Eoghan, G., *Ireland in Prehistory,* Routledge and Kegan Paul, London, 1977, p. 76.
3 Edwards, Nancy, *The Archaeology of Early Medieval Ireland*, Batsford, London, 1990, p. 170.
4 Leask, H.G., *Irish Castles,* Dundalgan Press, Dundalk, 1951, p. 106.
5 Murphy, Seamus, *Stone Mad,* Routledge and Kegan Paul, London, 1966, p. 178

Chapter 3: Equipment, Men & Commerce
1 O'Kelly, M.J., 'Two ring-forts at Garryduff, Co. Cork', *Proceedings of the Royal Irish Academy*, series c, Dublin, 1963, pp. 46, 51.

2   Herity, M. and Eoghan, G., op. cit. p. 236.

3   Berger, Rainer, '^{14}C dating mortar in Ireland', *Radiocarbon*, vol. 34, no. 3, 1992, p. 884.

4   Deegan, Michael, 'The development of quarrying techniques', *Engineers' Journal*, Dublin, August 1960, p. 327.

5   Burgoyne, Gen. Sir J., *A Treatise on the Blasting and Quarrying of Stone for Building and other Purposes*, London, 1874, p. 3.

6   Killian, Tony, 'Blasting practice in Irish quarries: changing techniques 1945 to 2003', unpublished paper, 2004, p. 1.

7   Petrie, George, *The Ecclesiastical Architecture of Ireland*, Irish University Press, Shannon, 1970, p. 142.

8   Harvey, John, *The Medieval Architect*, Wayland, London, 1972, p. 14.

9   Ibid. p. 149.

10 Hayden, Martin, *The Book of Bridges*, Marshall Cavendish, London, 1976, p. 19.

11 Henry, Françoise, *Irish Art in the Early Christian Period*, Methuen and Co. Ltd., London, 1965, p. 19.

12 Ryan, N., 'Mason's marks on cut-stone at the Custom House, Dublin', *Journal of the Royal Society of Antiquaries*, vol. 119, Dublin, 1989, p. 127.

13 Hourihane, Colum, *The Mason and his Marks: Mason's Marks in the Medieval Irish Archbishoprics of Cashel and Dublin*, British Archaeological Reports, Oxford, 2002, p. 48.

14 Ryan, N., op. cit. pp. 131–3.

15 Harbison, P., '12th and 13th-century stonemasons in Regensburg (Bavaria)', *Studies*, Dublin, winter 1975, p. 336.

16 Byrne, Francis John, *Irish Kings and High Kings*, Batsford, London, 1973, p. 175.

17 Macalister, R.A.S., *The Secret Languages of Ireland*, Cambridge University Press, 1937, pp. 225–41.

18 Hazlet, W.C., *The Livery Companies of the City of London*, Swan Sonnenschien and Co., London, 1892. p. 565.

19 Webb, John J., *The Guilds of Dublin*, Kennikat Press, New York, 1929, p. 282.

20 Sloan, John, et al., *Rules of the Stonecutters' Union of Ireland*, Dublin, 1929, p. 5.

21 Gibney, Arthur, 'Studies in 18th-century building history', Ph.D. thesis, Trinity College, Dublin, 1997, p. 189.

22 Heyman, Jacques, *The Masonry Arch*, Ellis Horwood Limited, Chichester, 1982, p. 44.

23 Ibid. p. 45.

24 Ibid. p. 50.

25 Ibid. p. 46.
26 O'Keeffe, Peter and Simington, Tom, *Irish Stone Bridges,* Irish Academic Press, Dublin, 1991, p. 73.
27 Wyse, Jackson Patrick, *The Building Stones of Dublin,* Town House and Country House, Dublin, 1993, p. 15.
28 Davies, A.C., 'Roofing Belfast and Dublin, 1896–98', *Journal of the Economic and Social History Society of Ireland,* vol. iv , 1997, p. 27.

Chapter 4: Early Christian Period to the Thirteenth Century
1 O'Riordan, S.P and Foy, J.B., 'The excavation of Leacanabuaile stone fort', *Journal of the Cork Historical and Archaeological Society,* vol. xlvi, no. 164, July–December 1941, pp. 87–8.
2 Edwards, Nancy, op. cit. p. 26.
3 Ibid. p. 122.
4 Ibid. p. 124.
5 Henry, Françoise (1965), op. cit., p. 84
6 Edwards, Nancy, op. cit. p. 100.
7 Henry, Françoise, *Irish Art During the Viking Invasions,* Methuen and Co. Ltd., London, 1967, p. 47.
8 Manning, Conleth, in Smyth, A.P. (ed.), *Seanchas, Studies in Early and Medieval Archaeology, History and Literature in Honour of Francis J. Byrne,* Four Courts Press, Dublin, 2000, p. 41.
9 Henry, Françoise (1967), op. cit., p. 48.
10 Champneys, Arthur C., *Irish Ecclesiastical Architecture*, G. Bell and Sons Ltd., London, 1910, p. 41.
11 Lalor, Brian, *The Irish Round Tower,* The Collins Press, Cork, 1999, p. 60.
12 Henry, Françoise (1967), op. cit., p. 50.
13 Elliott, Marianne, *The Catholics of Ulster, A History*, Penguin, London, 2000, p. 31, quoting from Livingstone, *Monaghan Story,* p. 44.
14 Leask, H.G., *Irish Churches and Monastic Buildings,* vol. 2, Dundalgan Press, Dundalk, 1960.
15 Thomas, Avril, *The Walled Towns of Ireland,* vol. 1, Irish Academic Press, Dublin, 1992, p. 64.

Chapter 5: Black Death & Cannons
1 O'Keeffe, Peter and Simington, Tom, op. cit. p. 28.
2 Thomas, Avril, *The Walled Towns of Ireland,* vol. 2, Irish Academic Press, Dublin, 1992, p. 138.
3 Webb, John J., op. cit. p. 218.
4 Craig, Maurice, *The Architecture of Ireland from Earliest Times to 1880*, Batsford, London, 1982, p. 81.

5 Ibid. p. 96.

6 Leask (1951), op. cit. p. 96.

7 Ibid. p. 153.

8 Ibid. pp. 79–83.

9 Ibid. p. 45.

10 Thomas, Avril (vol. 1), op. cit. p. 109.

Chapter 6: Exit Earls, Enter Georgiana

1 Ibid. p. 116.

2 Thomas, Avril, *The Walled Towns of Ireland,* vol. 2, Irish Academic Press, Dublin, 1992, p. 155.

3 Kerrigan, Paul M., *Castles and Fortifications in Ireland 1485–1945,* The Collins Press, Cork, 1995, p. 7.

4 Mulloy, S., 'French engineers with the Jacobean army', *Irish Sword,* vol. xv, 1983., pp. 222–32.

5 Kerrigan, Paul. M., op. cit. p. 110.

6 Ibid. p. 155.

7 Craig, Maurice, op. cit. p. 248.

8 Vallancy, C., *A Practical Treatise on Stonecutting,* T. Ewing, Dublin, 1766.

9 Semple, G., *A Treatise on Building in Water,* J.A. Husband, Dublin, 1776.

10 Cullen, L.M., 'Eighteenth-century flour milling in Ireland', *Journal of the Irish Economic and Social History Society,* vol. iv, 1997, pp. 5–25.

11 Young, Arthur, *Tour of Ireland 1776–9,* London, 1780.

12 Burke, John F., *Outlines of the Industrial History of Ireland,* Brown and Nolan, Dublin, 1933, p. xi.

13 Semple, G., op. cit. p. 55.

14 de Courcy, J.W., *The Liffey in Dublin,* Gill and Macmillan, Dublin, 1996, p. 377.

15 Cox, R.C. and Gould, M.H., *Civil Engineering Heritage,* Thomas Telford Publications, London, 1998, p. 18.

16 Ibid. p. 24.

17 Ibid. p. 237.

18 McCutcheon, W.A., *The Industrial Archaeology of Northern Ireland,* HMSO, Belfast, 1980, pp. 53–8.

19 Cox, R.C. and Gould, M.H., op. cit. p. 109.

Chapter 7: Famine, Science & Commerce

1 Daly, Mary E., *The Buffer State,* Institute of Public Administration, Dublin, 1997, p. 16.

2 McAfee, Patrick, *Irish Stone Walls,* The O'Brien Press, Dublin, 1997, pp. 42–7.
3 Wilkinson, G., *Practical Geology and Ancient Architecture of Ireland,* William Curry and Co., Dublin, 1845.
4 Kerrigan, Paul. M., op. cit. p. 172.
5 Ibid. p. 159.
6 Ibid. p. 14.
7 Cox, R.C. and Gould, M.H., op. cit. p. 28.
8 McCutcheon, W.A., *The Industrial Archaeology of Northern Ireland,* HMSO, Belfast, 1980, p. 69.
9 Ibid. p. 70.
10 Ibid. p. 293.
11 Hogg, William E., *The Millers and the Mills of Ireland about 1850,* W.E. Hogg, Dublin, 1997, p. 42.
12 Cox, R.C. and Gould, M.H., op. cit. p. 85.
13 Craig, Maurice, op. cit. p. 210.
14 Cox, R.C. and Gould, M.H., op. cit. p. 17.
15 Ochshorn, Jonathan, 'Stone in 20th-century architecture', 2004, at www.people.cornell/edu/pages/comments/stone.html

Chapter 8: Mechanisation & Heritage

1 Ibid.
2 Pegun, Caroline, *Building for Government: The Architecture of State Buildings OPW: Ireland 1900–2000,* Town House and Country House, Dublin, 1999, pp. 240–1.
3 O'Connor, Kevin, *Ironing the Land,* Gill and Macmillan, Dublin, 1999, p. 96.
4 Benson, Gordon, 'Millennium Wing, National Gallery of Ireland', *Irish Architect*, Dublin, March 2002, p. 16.

Appendix: An Gobán Saor

1 O'Hógán D., *Myth, Legend, Romance,* Ryan Publishing, London, 1990, p. 241.
2 Petrie, George, op. cit. p. 385.
3 Kelly, F., op. cit. pp. 21–28.
4 O'Curry, E., *The Manners and Customs of the Ancient Irish,* William & Norgate, London, 1873, p. 46.
5 Brash, Richard R., 'Notes on the ancient ecclesiastical architecture of Ireland', *The Irish Builder*, 1 March 1874, p. 68.
6 Ibid. p. 69.

Bibliography

Bartlett, T. and Jeffrey, K. (eds.), *A Military History of Ireland*, Cambridge University Press, 1996.

Benson, Gordon, 'Millennium Wing, National Gallery of Ireland', *Irish Architect*, Dublin, March 2002, pp. 13–24.

Berger, Rainer, '14C dating mortar in Ireland', *Radiocarbon*, vol. 34, no. 3, 1992, pp. 880–9.

Berry, H.F., 'The Dublin Guild of Carpenters, Millers, Masons and Heliers in the sixteenth century', *Dublin Historical Record,* vol. xii, November 1952, pp. 120–5.

Brash, Richard R., 'Notes on the ancient ecclesiastical architecture of Ireland', *The Irish Builder*, 1 March 1874.

Burgoyne, Gen. Sir J., *A Treatise on the Blasting and Quarrying of Stone for Building and other Purposes*, London, 1874.

Burke, John F., *Outlines of the Industrial History of Ireland*, Brown and Nolan, Dublin, 1933.

Byrne, Francis John, *Irish Kings and High Kings,* Batsford, London, 1973.

Champneys, Arthur C., *Irish Ecclesiastical Architecture*, G. Bell and Sons Ltd., London, 1910.

Cox, R.C. and Gould, M.H., *Civil Engineering Heritage*, Thomas Telford Publications, London, 1998.

Cox, R.C. and Gould, M.H., *Ireland's Bridges*, Wolfhound Press, Dublin, 2003.

Cullen, L.M., 'Eighteenth-century flour milling in Ireland', *Journal of the Irish Economic and Social History Society*, vol. iv (1997), pp. 5–25.

Craig, Maurice, *The Architecture of Ireland from Earliest Times to 1880*, Batsford, London, 1982.

Daly, Mary E., *The Buffer State*, Institute of Public Administration, Dublin, 1997.

Davies, A.C., 'Roofing Belfast and Dublin, 1896–98', *Journal of the Economic and Social History Society of Ireland,* vol. iv (1997), pp. 26–35.

De Breffny, Brian and Mott, George, *The Churches and Abbeys of Ireland,* Thames and Hudson, London, 1976.

de Courcy, J.W., *The Liffey in Dublin,* Gill & Macmillan, Dublin, 1996.

Deegan, Michael, 'The Development of quarrying techniques', *Engineers' Journal,* Dublin, August 1960.

Edwards, Nancy, *The Archaeology of Early Medieval Ireland,* Batsford, London, 1990.

Elliott, Marianne, *The Catholics of Ulster: A History,* Penguin, London, 2000.

Feely, Barry, 'Limestone quarries', *Proceedings of Seminar on Irish Stone organised by Geological Survey of Ireland and the Architectural and Monumental Stone Association,* Dublin, 1986.

Finlay, I., *Celtic Art,* Faber & Faber, London, 1973.

Gibney, Arthur, 'Studies in 18th-century building history', Ph.D. thesis, Trinity College, Dublin, 1997.

Harbison, P., '12th and 13th-century stonemasons in Regensburg (Bavaria)', *Studies,* Dublin, winter 1975.

Harvey, John, *The Medieval Architect,* Wayland, London, 1972.

Hayden, Martin, *The Book of Bridges,* Marshall Cavendish, London, 1976.

Hazlet, W.C., *The Livery Companies of the City of London,* Swan Sonnenschien & Co., London, 1892.

Heyman, Jacques, *The Masonry Arch,* Ellis Horwood Ltd., Chichester, 1982.

Henry, Françoise, *Irish Art in the Early Christian Period,* Methuen & Co. Ltd., London, 1965.

Henry, Françoise, *Irish Art During the Viking Invasions,* Methuen & Co. Ltd., London, 1967.

Herity, M. and Eoghan, G., *Ireland in Prehistory,* Routledge & Kegan Paul, London, 1977.

Hogg, William E., *The Millers and the Mills of Ireland about 1850,* W.E. Hogg, Dublin, 1997.

Hourihane, Colum, *The Mason and his Marks: Mason's Marks in the Medieval Irish Archbishoprics of Cashel and Dublin,* British Archaeological Reports, Oxford, 2002.

Jackson, Dr John, 'History of stone', *Proceedings of Seminar on Irish Stone organised by Geological Survey of Ireland and the Architectural and Monumental Stone Association,* Dublin, 1986.

Kearns, Hugh, *The Mysterious Chequered Lights of Newgrange,* Elo Publications, Dublin, 1993.

Kelly, E., *Ireland's Master Storyteller,* Marino Books, Dublin, 1998.

Kelly, F., *A Guide to Early Irish Law,* Dublin, 1988.

Kerrigan, Paul M., *Castles and Fortifications in Ireland 1485–1945,* The Collins Press, Cork, 1995.

Killian, Tony, 'Blasting practice in Irish quarries: changing techniques, 1945 to 2003', unpublished paper, 2004.

Lalor, Brian, *The Irish Round Tower,* The Collins Press, Cork, 1999.

London County Council, *Construction Bylaws, part iv,* London, 1937.

Leask, H.G., *Irish Castles,* Dundalgan Press, Dundalk, 1951.

Leask, H.G., *Irish Churches and Monastic Buildings,* vols. 1–3, Dundalgan Press, Dundalk, 1960.

Lucas, A.T., *Treasures of Ireland,* Gill & Macmillan, Dublin, 1973.

McAfee, Patrick, *Irish Stone Walls,* The O'Brien Press, Dublin, 1997.

Macalister, R.A.S., *The Secret Languages of Ireland,* Cambridge University Press, 1937.

McCutcheon, W.A., *The Industrial Archaeology of Northern Ireland,* HMSO, Belfast, 1980.

MacNeill, E., *Ancient Irish Law,* PRIA, 36c, 1923.

Manning, Conleth, in Smyth, A.P. (ed.) *Seanchas, Studies in Early and Medieval Archaeology, History and Literature in Honour of Francis J. Byrne,* Four Courts Press, Dublin, 2000.

Mulloy, S., 'French engineers with the Jacobean army', *Irish Sword,* vol. xv, 1983.

Murphy, Seamus, *Stone Mad,* Routledge & Kegan Paul, London, 1966.

Nowlan, Kevin B. (ed.), *Travel and Transport in Ireland,* Gill & Macmillan, Dublin, 1973.

O'Connell, J.W. and Korff, A., *The Book of the Burren,* Tír Eolas, Kinvara, County Galway, 2001.

O'Connor, Kevin, *Ironing the Land,* Gill & Macmillan, Dublin, 1999.

O'Curry, E., *The Manners and Customs of the Ancient Irish,* William & Norgate, London, 1873.

O'Hógán D., *Myth, Legend, Romance,* Ryan Publishing, London, 1990.

O'Keeffe, Peter and Simington, Tom, *Irish Stone Bridges,* Irish Academic Press, Dublin, 1991.

O'Kelly, M.J., 'Two ring-forts at Garryduff, Co. Cork', *Proceedings of the Royal Irish Academy,* series c, Dublin, 1963.

O'Kelly, M.J., *Newgrange, Archaeology, Art and Legend,* Thames and Hudson, 1982.

O'Kelly, M.J., *Early Ireland,* Cambridge University Press, 1989.

Ochshorn, Jonathan, 'Stone in 20th-century architecture', 2004, at www.people.cornell/edu/pages/comments/stone.html

O'Riordan, S.P and Foy, J.B., 'The excavation of Leacanabuaile stone fort', *Journal of the Cork Historical and Archaeological Society,* vol. xlvi, no. 164, July–December 1941.

O'Sullivan, Dr M., *Megalithic Art in Ireland,* Town House and Country House, Dublin, 1993.

Pavia, Sara and Bolton, Jason, *Stone, Brick and Mortar,* Wordwell Ltd., Wicklow, 2000.

Pegun, Caroline, *Building for Government: The Architecture of State Buildings OPW: Ireland 1900–2000,* Town House and Country House, Dublin, 1999.

Petrie, George, *The Ecclesiastical Architecture of Ireland,* Irish University Press, Shannon, 1970.

Rothery, Seán, *A Field Guide to the Buildings of Ireland,* The Lilliput Press, Dublin, 1997.

Ryan, N., 'Mason's marks on cut-stone at the Custom House, Dublin', *Journal of the Royal Society of Antiquaries,* vol. 119, Dublin, 1989.

Sloan, John, et al., *Rules of the Stonecutters' Union of Ireland,* Dublin, 1929.

Semple, G., *A Treatise on Building in Water,* J.A. Husband, Dublin, 1776.

Thomas, Avril, *The Walled Towns of Ireland,* vols. 1–2, Irish Academic Press, Dublin, 1992.

Thomas, N.L., *Irish Symbols of 3500 BC,* Mercier Press, Cork, 1988.

Vallancy, C., *A Practical Treatise on Stonecutting,* T. Ewing, Dublin, 1766.

Webb, John J., *The Guilds of Dublin,* Kennikat Press, New York, 1929.

Wilkinson, G., *Practical Geology and Ancient Architecture of Ireland,* William Curry & Co., Dublin, 1845.

Wyse, Jackson Patrick, *The Building Stones of Dublin,* Town House and Country House, Dublin, 1993.

Young, Arthur, *Tour of Ireland 1776–9,* London, 1780.

Index